Jump rope!

Five, ten, fifteen, twenty,
Nobody leaves the jump-rope empty.
If they do, they shall suffer:
Take an end and be a duffer!

Jump rope!

by Peter L. Skolnik

Photographs by Jerry Darvin

Illustrations by Marty Norman

wp Workman Publishing Co., New York

ISBN: 0-911104-47-X

Workman Publishing Company
231 East 51st Street
New York, New York 10022

First printing October 1974

Design by Paul Hanson
Illustrations by Marty Norman
Photographs by Jerry Darvin

Typeset by Trade Composition
Printed and bound by the George Banta Company

Manufactured in the United States of America

For my daughter Samantha, for whom I will always be a steady ender

P.S. 75, New York City

Rye Country Day School, Rye, New York

Manzanita School, Oakland, California

P.S. 144, New York City

Several people helped me create this book in one way or another, and I thank them all—Jennifer, Peter, Ann, Sally, Sarah, Debbie, Viola and Gabe Paul. And my special thanks to Dr. Robert C. Darling, Steve Maletz, and the kids and administrators of the Rye Country Day School, the Manzanita School, P.S. 75, and P.S. 144.

JUMP FOR JOY!!!
1776.   1876.

CRANDALL'S
CENTENNIAL JUMPING ROPE.
PATENTED, NOVEMBER 9th, 1875.

This novel invention is the only known improvement on the old jumping-rope. It must be seen to be appreciated. *With a little practice a child can become skillful in its use and find graceful movement, healthful exercise and amusement.* Send for Circular.

Contents

Introduction

Everyone jumps rope. Or, perhaps, everyone *has* jumped rope—whether as a childhood passion, a temporary diversion, or a momentary collapse in a backbone of propriety. I would offer tempting odds that there is not an able-bodied man, woman, or child who has not, at some time or another, succumbed to the challenging fascination of a turning rope.

What you probably didn't realize is that there is a whole world of jump-rope. Sure, it's a world of school kids and playgrounds, but it's also a world of ball players and boxers, cardiac patients and overweights. And most important, it's becoming a world of busy housewives, active career girls, sedentary office workers, and flabby executives who want to get in shape and stay that way.

This wealth of activity called jump-rope—a cornucopia of games, rhymes, contests and exercises—springs from the simple child's pastime you first thought of when you read the words JUMP ROPE! on the cover. As a kid's game, whether it's called jump-rope, skip-rope, or skipping, the excitement generated by a twirling hunk of clothesline, grapevine, or leather thong has been increasingly restricted to the girls' corner of the playgrounds and back lots of America. This was not always so, here or elsewhere.

Actually, most evidence suggests that this pastime is "probably very ancient" and was originally a boys' game. As a matter of fact, upstart little tomboys of the 1850's were warned about "instances of blood vessels burst by young ladies who, in a silly attempt to jump a certain number of hundred times, have persevered in jumping after their strength was exhausted.'' What could possibly be more unladylike than collapsing in a bloody heap right there on the front lawn!

But with the approach of the twentieth century came less frilly girls' dresses, improvements in rough playgrounds, and mass movements of populations toward the bustling cities. Girls were encouraged to play more actively, to develop agility and grace. They were sent off to ballet schools in droves. And with their new-found confidence in the pirouette, they began to abandon the sedate storytelling of their singing games for the more exhilarating pleasures of the jump-rope.

It wasn't long before the game skyrocketed to first place on a very long list of favorite girls' activities—a position which it has held ever since. But as the girls enlisted, the boys began moving off into organized sports like baseball, football, and basketball. Suddenly jump-rope, this former proving ground for young men with athletic pretensions, had become sissy stuff. It was ''for the girls,'' which was considerably more horrifying than ''for the birds.''

My own best guess is that the rhymes helped keep the boys away. Rhymes were introduced by girls to structure the game noncompetitively. But boys have always been encouraged to compete, and this is what they look for in their games. Also, the rhymes tended to be a bit threatening to young masculinity, concerned as they were with fantasies and amorous pursuits.

But now it's 1974. Girls are batting clean-up for the local Little League and jockeying for position in the Preakness, while Muhammad Ali teaches Dick Cavett to jump-rope. Today there is a new emphasis on competition in jump-rope, with some new ''rhymes'' which are little more than simple rhythmic reminders or instructions to the jumpers. This has all led to a renewed premium on the traditionally male attributes of endurance, stamina, and agility.

Gentlemen, you may take up your ropes unafraid. M. Ali would approve.

Bluebells: A rope which sways gently from side to side but does not go over the jumper's head, as in "Rock the Cradle"-type games, and the beginning of many versions of the rhyme "Bluebells, cockle shells." See WAVIE.

Bullets: Fast turning. This term was common in the fifties but less so now. See also HOT PEPPER, HOT PEAS, WHIPPING, RED HOT BRICKS.

Bumps: An advanced action where the rope passes under the feet twice in one jump. Also known as FIREYS. See the game "Bumps" and its accompanying rhymes.

Call In—Call Out: A type of game or rhyme where jumpers are chosen by another player already jumping to join or follow into the rope.

Continues! (Continuation): A cry by the jumper which permits him or her to continue jumping after a trip or a miss. Often the "continuation" jumping will be of a harder variety, such as HOT PEPPER or HIGH WATERS. For examples of "continuation" in action, see the games "Bumps" and "Partners Double-Dutch."

Crossie: A solo game where the arms cross at the elbows as the rope descends, creating a wide loop to jump through. The arms uncross as the rope comes up behind. Robert Louis Stevenson, in *Notes on the Movements of Young Children* (1874), describes a girl performing a trick "in which she crossed her hands before her with a motion not unlike weaving."

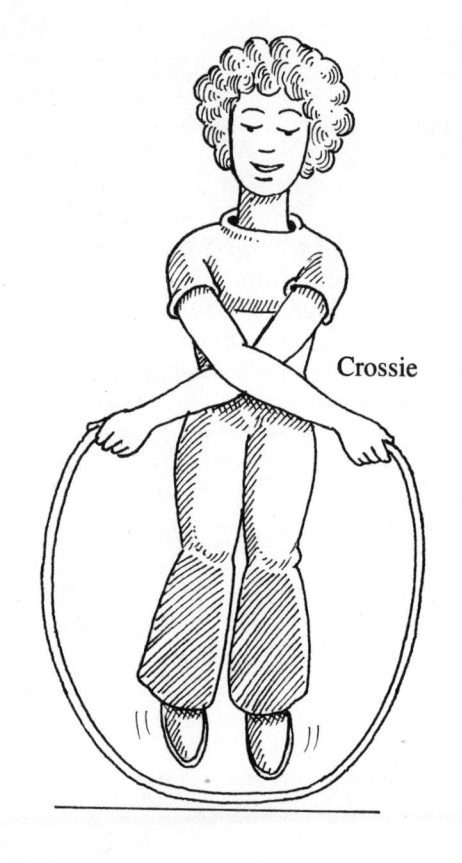

Crossie

Dead Rope: Competition term for a still rope, before the starter's signal.

Dolly: A stunt where the turners circle around the jumper. See the game "High, Low, Dolly, Pepper."

Rope talk

A Glossary of Jump-Rope Terms

Back Door

Like most games with a world-wide following, jump-rope has a language of its own. But "Double Orange" in Manhattan may be "Double Irish" in Indiana and, for that matter, "Scotch" on the other side of the Brooklyn Bridge. Rope talk can present some knotty problems, but here is an attempt to untangle them.

Back Door: Running in to a turning rope which, as it hits the ground, rises *toward* the jumper. The player must jump *as she enters*—a tricky maneuver. In Scotland this is known as entry from the "dykie (wall) side" of the rope. See also FRONT DOOR, OVER THE MOON.

Black Sheep: A novice. Black sheep never have to turn, or be out. See WHITE SHEEP.

25

sardine.'' When the professor's daughter got her turn at the rope she chanted, with innocent wisdom, ''And turn your back on the sour, sour Dean.'' She may not have been a canned-fish gourmet, but she knew who put the flies in Daddy's ointment.

The rhymes tend to be an intriguing blend of children's interpretations of the adult world and their own fantasies, unconscious desires, anxieties, and psychological graffiti. Rhymes have spread by word of mouth and personal contact on every level—from the early waves of immigrants arriving in America to wartime gatherings of servicemen's children, and summer camp and family visiting.

Most of the evidence suggests that few rhymes were used before the mid-nineteenth century, and that the proliferation of rhymes is largely a metropolitan phenomenon of the present century. American sources of the 1880's list a grand total of four jump-rope rhymes, including early versions of ''Down in the meadow where the green grass grows'' and ''I like coffee, I like tea.''

But all of the earliest rhymes which found their

rhymes. These are the very stuff of folklore and have been recorded and analyzed ad nauseam. Indeed, library shelves abound with dusty folklore journals containing innumerable unread articles on jump-rope rhymes. After years of public indifference, someone has finally found the courage and massive will power to wade through these forgotten volumes. I alone am escaped to tell thee.

By and large, the rhymes are not, and were not, written by children. Nor, I am delighted to report, by adults. Rather, like Topsy, they grew. Lucy Nulton, writing in the *Journal of American Folklore*, vol. 61, has provided a comprehensive explanation of the characteristics of jump-rope rhymes as folk literature.

"As in all true folk literature, these rhymes come from the people, travel by spoken word, portray the world and affairs of the common folk, develop variations through usage, deal with the elemental, often have a fundamental truth in them, exhibit subtleties of characterization, reflect social mores, show the growth of living language, and endure as tradition. . . . They become varied in form, accompanying action, idiom, implications, and rhythm, according to fancy, previous experiences, vocabulary, and misunderstandings of the jumpers and chanters."

Perhaps it is these "misunderstandings" which provide the most delightfully absurd variations. One of my favorite jump-rope stories is about the five-year-old daughter of a Seattle college professor. The older girls at the annual faculty picnic were skipping happily to "Charlie Chaplin went to France," including the local version of the concluding couplet—"S'lute to the King, and bow to the Queen,/ And turn your back on the sour

Rope lore

Jump-Rope History

Game historians have suggested that young boys shot marbles in the shadow of the Sphinx, that kids played tag while Mark Antony borrowed some ears around the corner, and that Socrates put a new tail on his nephew's kite without even asking why.

If the scholars continue to hunt down some concrete evidence that jump-rope was around before the 1600's (notice the fellow in the mid-right of the illustration on p.16), it's a safe bet they will find what they are looking for.

As with all kids' games, the underlying origin of the activity of jump-rope is the subject of much hard-boiled scholarly conjecture. In 1929, Henry Bett writing in *The Games of Children: Their Origin and History* had a more romantic and appealing notion than most.

"It may be significant that skipping . . . prevails during the spring months of the year–the months when the seed is springing up . . . . There is a custom widely distributed in the world . . . by which those who are sowing seed leap as high as they can at every few steps, that the hemp or the flax may grow as high as they leap . . . . When our children nowadays skip . . . as a game they are in the line of descent from a very ancient magical custom."

Scholars may remain unconvinced. But I'll give Mr. Bett four gold jump-ropes for creative thinking.

We walk on slightly firmer ground when we explore the background of the accompanying

In MGM's "*Sunday Punch*," Lana Turner shows Dan Daily and Bill Lundigan how to stay in shape.

way to the jump-rope arena derived, wholesale or piecemeal, from existing sources—singing games of the "Ring Around the Rosy" variety, the Elizabethan flower oracles quoted by Shakespeare's mad Ophelia, the counting-out rhymes of the "Eenie, meenie, miny, mo" family—and a bit of the creative outpouring of that most poetic of birds, Mother Goose.

In the cities, kids of the same age and interests were brought into far closer and more frequent contact with each other than their country cousins had enjoyed. Solo turns of one child with one rope—jumping for speed, endurance, or mastery of a new stunt—became old hat. The new craze was a group game with "enders" turning for a line of eager players. It was not very long before the singing games, counting-out rhymes, and folk ballads learned at mother's knee and the political doggerel heard on every street corner were shared, combined, transformed, altered, and edited. The resulting hybrid ditties, a children's communal art form, provided an intoxicating rhythm for the enders to turn to and the jumpers to jump to The jump-rope rhyme had come of age.

Jump-rope is an active game, providing physical exercise and release. But through the added feature of the rhymes, with hundreds of existing examples and endless possibilities, it provides emotional and psychological release as well. The constrained citizens of past centuries used the sheltering wing of Mother Goose to express the otherwise unspeakable truth of political and social tyranny.

In the same way, the small citizens of Kids Kingdom today have found the jump-rope rhyme a safe way to let out their innermost frustrations, confusions, concerns, and wonderfully tolerant criticisms of the world around them.

Bothersome baby brother, amorous big sister, stern parents, teacher, preacher, and crazy Mrs. Brown across the street—all get their comeuppance. The jump-rope rhyme is the medium, and the message is there for anyone who hears or reads it.

JUMPING ROPE.

This play should likewise be used with caution. It is a healthy exercise, and tends to make the form graceful; but it should be used with moderation. I have known instances of blood vessels burst by young ladies, who, in a silly attempt to jump a certain number of hundred times, have persevered in jumping after their strength was exhausted. There are several ways of jumping a rope:

1. Simply springing and passing the rope under the feet with rapidity.

2. Crossing arms at the moment of throwing the rope.

3. Passing the rope under the feet of two or three.

In "Double with a Third," which sounds a lot like "Chase," the crouch word is "Third."

> I said a double,
> With
> A
> Third
> I said a double
> With
> A
> Third
> etc.

High, Low, Dolly, Pepper: This game is fun because it has some built-in suspense for the jumpers. Each player runs in and jumps while the words "high," "low," "dolly," "pepper" are repeated. Your stunt is determined by the word you miss on. "High" is HIGH WATERS [rope turned at about knee level] "Low" is LOW WATERS [Jumper crouches and jumps a low rope]. "Dolly" indicates jumping in a circle while crouching *or* jumping in place while the *enders move in a circle*. PEPPER, of course, is fast turning. Players can do their stunts either when they first miss or in a separate round.

D-i-s-h Choice: This popular New York game is very much like "High, Low, Dolly, Pepper," but offers a few more options. Players repeat the phrase "D, I, S, H, Choice" until they miss, and choose their stunt accordingly. I have seen the entire game played to DOUBLE DUTCH turning, including the stunts. Want a challenge? Try jumping Double Dutch on one foot.

D, I, S, H, CHOICE.
D = DOUBLE DUTCH or DOUBLE ORANGE
I = Irish [one rope on ground; step over]
Indian [jump with a "war -whoop"]
S = Statute [jump with body stiff]
Steps [high stepping]
Sleep [eyes closed; head on hands]
H = Hop on one foot
CHOICE = Any of the above.

Exams: Another game which is fun for enders and is the jump-rope equivalent of Giant Steps. The teachers [ENDERS] decide upon an exam to give the players.

The exams may be identical or different for each player. A typical exam might include 8 HIGH WATERS, 5 BLUEBELLS, and 6 PEPPERS. The teachers announce the course, and count aloud as each student takes the test.

Skim The Milk: This is a stunt marathon. To "skim the milk" refers to a complete run-through of Steps 1–5.

1. Run in, jump once, run out.
2. Run in, jump twice, run out.
3. Run in, jump 3 times, run out.
4. Run in, jump 4 times, run out.
5. Run in, jump 5 times, run out.

The "skimming" may be varied in many ways. Here are suggestions.

a. Skim the milk front door.
b. Skim the milk back door.

word out loud while performing certain actions with her hands or feet:

1. M(split), I(hop), S(wobbly-legs), S(wobbly-legs),
   I(hop), S(wobbly-legs), S(wobbly-legs), I(hop).
   P(touch the ground), P(touch the ground), I(hop).

2.

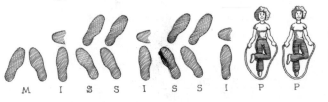

3. The third way uses a rhyme and a pantomime as varied as the imagination of the jumper:

This is the way you spell Mississippi.
Capital M, I, crooked-letter,
    crooked-letter, I,
Crooked-letter, crooked-letter, I,
Hunchback, hunchback, I!

Baby In The Cradle: This is an action-rhyme-game in which OVER THE WATER alternates with regular jumping. Players run in and kneel beneath the spinning rope until the first "One, two, three." The rope then turns normally until the last "One,

two, three," when the jumper runs out and the next player runs in and kneels beneath the rope.

Baby in the cradle, [kneeling]
Playing with the ladle.
One, two, three. [full turning]

Andy Pandy,
Sugarallie-Andy.
One, two, three. [next player enter and
                  kneel]

A shorter version dates from 1910.

Andy Pandy, sugary candy.
French almond NUTS!

At "NUTS!," which is screamed with glass-shattering intensity, the player crouches and the rope is spun above the head as the words are repeated rapidly. Alternate jumping and crouching.

One Way, Two Way: Two other rhyme-games which require the player to crouch under a spinning rope are played in New York, but may have come from the Caribbean islands where this kind of jumping is very common. In "One Way, Two Way," the rope spins above the head on the word "way."

One way.
Two way.
Three way.
etc.

Double Dutch: The most common two-rope game, and a term which has been in widespread use since the turn of the century. Most often DOUBLE DUTCH indicates that both ropes are turning *inward* in an eggbeater motion, and that the turners are using an overhand action. The other common two-rope game requires that both ropes turn *outward,* and the turners use an underhand motion. The outward form is far more difficult, since it requires a high step and a wide side-to-side movement while jumping to clear the ropes alternately.

Two ropes both turning *inward* is known as DOUBLE DUTCH in New York, St. Louis, San Francisco, Philadelphia, Nebraska, Indiana, and most of the other states, as it was in the British Isles in the 1890's. But this same form has been reported as DOUBLE FRENCH (Oregon), DOUBLE

ROPE (Texas), DUTCH ROPE (New York, 1920), FRENCH (New Zealand), FRENCH ROPES (Scotland), THE EGGBEATER among physical education teachers and, quite simply, JUMPING TWO ROPES in North Carolina.

The more difficult game of jumping two ropes turning *outward* is not as common under any name, but it is known as DOUBLE IRISH in Philadelphia and Fort Wayne, SCOTCH in the Brownsville section of Brooklyn, DOUBLE ORANGE in Harlem, and was called FRENCH DUTCH in the back alleys of London in 1898.

The two-rope games are the ultimate test of the jumper's art. The competitive "Partners Double Dutch" is, for my money, more exciting than any cricket match on record.

Duck Skipping: Jumping in a crouched position.

Double Dutch

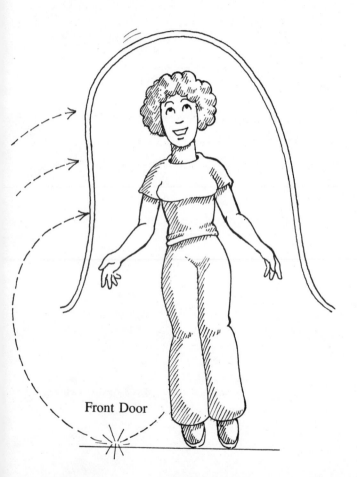

Front Door

Enders: Those who turn the rope. Generally not an enviable job, but there are some who enjoy it and are quickly recruited as STEADY ENDERS by their group. When no one volunteers, kids have shown typical ingenuity at passing out the dirty work. See LOOPS.

In most games a jumper who trips or otherwise fails to complete his or her turn must relieve one of the enders. "Exams" and "Sweet Stuff Shop" are two games in which the ender's role is more desirable.

A few blocks from my home, during jump-rope season, an elderly Puerto Rican woman reports to the play street promptly at noon on each school day. Armed with her own rope, she is perhaps the oldest steady ender in recorded history. I think the Guinness people should investigate.

Fireys: See BUMPS.

French, French Dutch, and French Ropes: See DOUBLE DUTCH.

Front Door: Running in to a turning rope which, as it hits the ground, rises *away from* the jumper. This is the easier, more common entry. The jumper has a moment to get set while the rope completes its arc. Scottish girls call this the "Plainie Side." See BACK DOOR, OVER THE MOON.

High Water(s): A term with three distinct meanings.

1. A turning rope which does not touch the ground, requiring a high jump. Generally the HIGH WATERS rope is from six inches to one foot off the ground, and may be raised gradually.

2. A rope spun above a crouching player's head. The player does not jump the HIGH WATER turns, which usually alternate with full turns. See OVER THE WATER, and the action games "One Way, Two Way," and "Baby In The Cradle."

3. An elimination game, more commonly called "High Water, Low Water," in which a taut non-turning rope is gradually raised as the line of players attempt to jump over it.

Hopsies: Jumping on one foot alone, while the other foot is raised and slightly bent at the knee. Also called HOPSIES ON ONE FOOT, HOPPIE, and HOPPIE ON ONE LEG.

Hot Peas: Fast turning, especially in the Southern United States and in some parts of New York City, where it is sometimes called HOT PEAS WITH BUTTER and occasionally HOT TAMALES.

Hot Pepper: The most common American term for a fast-turning rope. Pennsylvania kids often call this RED HOT PEPPER. Jumpers in Wisconsin, seemingly out of the mainstream, call fast turning RED HOT BRICKS and *really* fast turning VINEGAR, which has a similar meaning in France, but generally indicates an intermediate speed in the United States.

In some places, HOT PEPPER is mercilessly applied to anyone who is outjumping their welcome.

Jumping Two Ropes: See DOUBLE DUTCH.

Keep The Kettle Boiling: See ON TIME.

Kiss: A touching of the two ropes in double-rope games. This accident is attributed to the enders, and the jumper is graciously permitted to begin again.

Licking: Slow, high turning, as in HIGH WATER 1. LICKING and SCOLDING have the same meaning and either one may be used in the last line of the game "Report Card." In Colorado LICKING is equated with HOT PEPPER. See the rhyme "Sitting on the Corner."

Loops: A way to determine the first enders. The rope is wound in loops and each player seizes one. When the rope is unwound, those holding the ends keep them.

A similar procedure involves doubling the rope over and passing it around a circle until someone can't double it anymore. This is repeated to determine misery's company.

Another way: the jumpers simply shout "First no enders!" at the beginning of play. He who hesitates is lost.

Low Waters: A rope which is turned low over a player who jumps in a crouch. Not to be confused with OVER or UNDER THE WATER, or HIGH WATERS 2, in which the player does not jump but simply stoops beneath a spinning rope.

Mustard: An intermediate speed, between SALT and PEPPER. See also VINEGAR.

Old Maid: In some of the prediction rhymes where the letters of the alphabet are jumped to determine a boyfriend's initial, a girl who jumps through without missing is stigmatized as an OLD MAID. This is a clever way of breaking down the good jumpers, who would rather name their heartthrobs than resign themselves to a life of solitude.

One Hundred: It is, in certain locales, considered bad luck to jump to 100. This is also a good ploy to guard against getting stuck as an ender while some ace player jumps to 18,000.

On Time: Games or rhymes in which the line of jumpers must enter the turning rope in a steady rhythm, never leaving the rope empty. This is the basic principle of timing games like "Chase," and "Five, Four, Three, Twenty-one."

Out My Window: Gracefully cutting short your turn by leaving before you miss. Perhaps the true test of jump-rope savoir-faire.

Over The Moon: Back door. UNDER THE MOON is, quite reasonably, front door.

Over The Water: This and its alternate term UNDER THE WATER both indicate a stunt where the rope spins quickly above the head of a crouching player, who does not jump. See HIGH WATER 2.

Pass The Baker: An early (1890's) British term which describes two jumpers changing places in the rope, crossing from left to right, and vice versa.

Pennies: An ender's cry which declares that when you are relieved of your end by an unsuccessful jumper you may enter the rope right away, without going to the back of the line. Of course, NO PENNIES! can be called by those on line or at the beginning of play, thus eliminating one of the last shreds of an ender's joy.

Pepper: See HOT PEPPER.

Red Hot Bricks: *Really* fast turning, as reported from Wisconsin. See HOT PEPPER.

Rope Types: It is predictable that in a game played around the world, various and sundry materials would be used as a "rope." Clothesline is, of course, accessible and popular. In an age when toy manufacturers have turned to plastic, #10 sash cord remains the "professional standard." Hopstems were employed by English children in the 1800's, while cow ropes were used in New Zealand. Kids in Spain jump with leather thongs, in Hungary with plaited straw, in Sweden with stiff wicker, and in France with string ropes woven on spool looms. Among the Cherokee Indians, jump-ropes of wild grapevines are common. Native vines make popular jump-ropes wherever they are found. In Barbados, both young bayvines and "rabbit vines" are soaked in tubs to keep them supple between uses.

Salt: Slow turning rope.

Scolding: See LICKING.

Scotch: See DOUBLE DUTCH.

Single Jumping: See STRAIGHT ROPE.

Skin: To jump as fast as you can until you miss.

Steady Enders: See ENDERS.

Straight Rope: Jumping a single rope or two ropes in a single strand turned by the enders to a strong single beat. The rhythms of DOUBLE DUTCH are faster, but not as insistent.

Turners: Those who *turn* the rope (North Carolina), *throw* the rope (Georgia), *swing* the rope (Minnesota), or *caw* the rope (British Isles and New Zealand). See ENDERS.

Up The Ladder: To move while jumping from one end or the center of the rope toward the other end. Jumping from one end of the rope to the other and returning *backwards* is moving UP AND DOWN THE LADDER.

Vinegar: VINEGAR and MUSTARD are intermediate speeds in most American jump-rope circles. However, in France VINEGAR refers to a fast rope (see HOT PEPPER), as it does in some parts of Wisconsin.

Wavie: A gently swaying rope which does not go over the jumper's head. This is a good way for a beginner to get used to the timing necessary for successful jumping. See also BLUEBELLS.

Whipping: Hard, fast turning, as in HOT PEPPER or HOT PEAS. See the game "Report Card."

White Sheep: An adept jumper. As opposed to the novice, BLACK SHEEP, the "whites" must take their turn at the ends, go out or to the end of the line when they miss, and generally abide by all the rules and regulations of the jump-rope flock they play with.

Rope how

Jump-Rope Technique

Jumping rope develops the ability to coordinate simultaneous movements of the hands and feet, which is not only necessary to all athletic skills, but comes in pretty handy for activities like dancing, playing the piano, driving a car, or squeezing through a closing subway door. It also develops balance, rhythm, and endurance. And, of course, it can help take off those few pounds of extra weight—particularly in the hips and thighs—while toning up muscles in other parts of the body, such as the arms, shoulders, and chest (giving added support to the bust).

But what is most significant, jumping rope can provide the same all-important conditioning of the heart, lungs, and circulatory system as jogging, running, swimming, or cycling. And what may be most appealing to the overweight or lazy, it can be done in the privacy of your home and at your own speed.

In this instructional section, we will deal with the fundamentals of solo jumping and interesting foot patterns you can use with the exercise programs in the next chapter. There are also specific tips for entering and jumping a rope being turned by others—the name of the game on the kids' circuit.

Ground Rules

The rope: The rope should be long enough to reach up under your arms when you stand on it. A slightly longer rope adds some degree of maneu-

Turning: Keep your upper arms fairly close to your sides, with the forearms out about a foot from your hips. Keep your wrists loose. Start with the rope behind your feet and swing it up over your head from behind to start it turning.

verability. You can, of course, buy a fancy rope with handles. But knots tied in the ends of a piece of clothesline will serve as well to help you maintain a comfortable grip, and knots are cheaper than handles every time. No. 10 sash-cord, available at your hardware store, is the recommended weight. But if they sell only 100-foot pieces for $8.50, don't feel obligated.

34

Jumping: You should only jump high enough to clear the turning rope—about one inch off the floor. Jump on the balls of the feet. In the beginning, a two-foot take-off when your feet leave the ground, and a two-foot landing are easiest. You should attempt to land in the same spot on each jump. Try to develop a bounce to your jumping, as this will provide an obvious rhythm and help you feel the timing of the turning of the rope. The "Rhythm Bounce" (see below) is a good way to do this.

Prepare for Take-Off

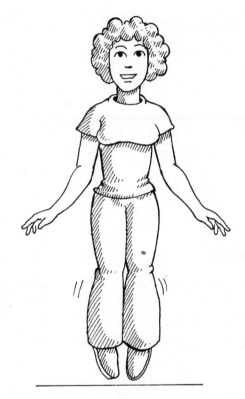

Practice the jumping movements *without* a rope at first.

1. Stand with your feet together, upper arms in, and hands about a foot out from the hips.

2. Bounce on the balls of your feet, an inch off the floor, at the rate of about 70 to 80 bounces per minute.

3. Keep your knees slightly bent, your hips loose, and try to land in approximately the same spot.

4. Jump for about 30 seconds, then rest.

5. Repeat steps 1 to 4 a few times.

Now practice turning movements *without* jumping.

6. Take both ends of the rope in one hand. Your hand should move in a 10-to-12 inch circle as the rope makes a circle parallel to your side and strikes the floor approximately 18 inches in front of your feet.

7. Practice the turning with each hand. Once you have the feel of both jumping and turning separately, combine them as follows.

8. Turn the rope a few times with one hand.

9. Keep turning and start bouncing in rhythm with the turning rope (but not jumping over it) for about 30 seconds. You should, of course, be jumping as the rope hits the floor.

10. Change hands and repeat.

11. Take the rope in both hands. Start in the basic position described above in Step 1. Try one turn and one jump a few times, then two turns and two jumps, then as many as possible.

Basic Bounces

These bounces can be used alone, or as part of the "fancy footwork" movements which can be combined into an interesting exercise program.

Plain bounce: Feet together, bounce once on each turn.

Rhythm bounce: Feet together, bounce twice on each turn—a 1-inch bounce as the rope passes under your feet, and a smaller bounce in between. As mentioned, this is a good way to get a feel for the rhythm of jumping.

Running bounce: Placing one foot in front of the other, run in place over the rope.

Release: The return to the basic feet-together position from *any* other foot position is called a release in the steps which follow.

Fancy Footwork

Turn the rope slowly when learning a new skill. Each step is done to one complete turn of the rope. The movements can be combined into various routines of your own devising to make an exercise program more interesting than endless single bouncing. They will also firm the legs, tone up the belly, and impress the friends and neighbors. Once you master these, you should have no problem improvising others.

Double Heel Hop

1. Plain bounce.
2. Bounce, landing with your weight on the ball of your left foot as you extend your right leg and

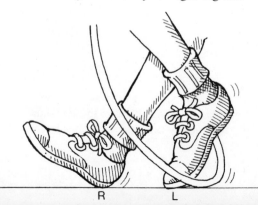

R   L

touch in front with the right heel. (Note: In all steps, both feet touch the floor *at the same time*. One foot carries the weight and the other touches lightly with heel or toe.)

3. Release (return to feet-together position).
4. Weight on your right foot as you touch in front with the left heel.
5. Release.

Double Toe Tap

1. Plain bounce.
2. Land on the left foot and touch behind you with right toe.

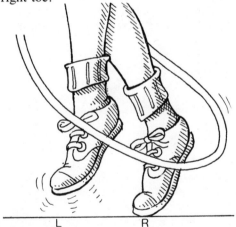

3. Release.
4. Land on the right foot and touch in back with the left toe.
5. Release.

Heel-To-Toe To-And-Fro

1. Plain bounce.
2. Land on left foot as you touch front with right heel.
3. Land on left foot again as you touch in back with right toe.
4. Repeat steps 2 and 3 several times.
5. Repeat, touching with left heel and toe, then combine in the Heel-To-Toe Double Whammy

Heel-To-Toe Double Whammy

1. Plain bounce.
2. Weight on the left foot and touch the right heel in front.
3. Weight on your left foot and touch the right toe in back.
4. Shift your weight to the right foot by landing on the ball of your right foot as you touch the left heel in front.
5. Land on your right foot and touch the left toe in back.
6. Shift weight to the left foot as you touch the right heel in front.
7. Continue from Step 3.

Heel-To-Toe Cross-As-You-Go

1. Plain bounce.
2. Weight on left foot and touch right heel front (or vice versa).

3. Land on left foot again as you cross right foot in front *over* left foot to touch right toe or vice versa.

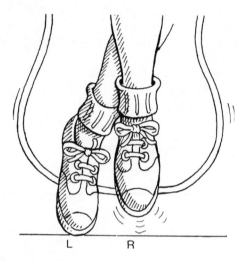

4. Land on left foot uncrossing feet, and touch — right heel in front again (or left heel if you've vice versa-ed).
5. Release.

Back-To-Back Thingumacrack

1. Plain bounce.
2. Land on left foot and touch right toe straight behind you.
3. Weight on left foot again and cross right foot over left foot *in back* to touch right toe.

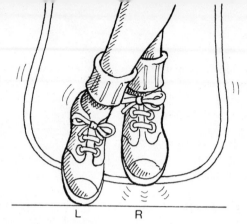

4. Land on left foot, uncross, and touch right toe straight behind again.
5. Release.

Heel-And-Toe Away-We-Go

1. Plain bounce.
2. Land on left foot as you touch in front with right heel.
3. Land on left foot as you cross right foot over in front and touch with right toe.
4. Land on left foot as you uncross right foot and touch front with right heel again.
5. Land on left foot as you touch with right toe straight in back.
6. Land on left foot as y ou cross right foot over in back and touch with right toe.
7. Land on left foot as you uncross right foot and touch with right toe straight in back.
8. Shift weight to right foot as you touch in front with left heel (landing with weight on ball of right foot).

9. Repeat, touching with left heel and toe (starting with Step 3).

Lovely Leg Spreads

1. Plain bounce.
2. Weight on left foot as you spread right leg 14 to 16 inches to the side, touching with toe.

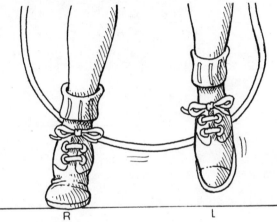

R   L

3. Release.
4. Repeat, spreading left leg to side.
5. Alternate, releasing between spreads.

Foot Flings

1. Plain bounce.
2. Land on the ball of the right foot leaning slightly to the left as you fling the left leg back and across behind the right leg.

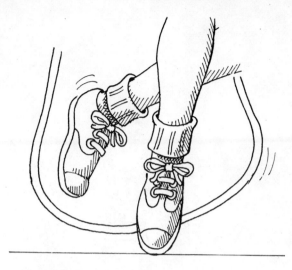

3. Release.
4. Repeat, landing on the left foot as you fling the right leg behind.

Tips on Jumping with Turners

Jumping while others turn the rope presents two basic problems—running in or out of the rope and, once in, coordinating your motion to the motion of the rope. Both of these problems require a ''feel'' for the timing of the turning rope, which you can obtain by *watching* the rope or by *listening* to the rope.

Most experienced jumpers can use both sight and sound to get into the rhythm of jumping. But younger children learn to rely on sight first. If you have trouble, listen to the sound the rope makes as it hits the ground. Stay relaxed, and try to hear and feel the rhythm.

Another good way to sense the rhythm of jumping is to have the turners sway the rope from side to side, but not over your head as you jump over it (BLUEBELLS). Gradually sway the rope more and more. Then when you feel the timing, jump over the rope as it turns fully over your head.

Remember, jump on the balls of both feet and don't jump too high—just enough for the rope to pass under you. Keep your feet spread comfortably and try to land in the same spot, near the middle of the rope. As you get closer to the turners, the rope gets lower and takes *less time* to make a full turn.

A two-foot take-off and two-foot landing are easiest. Some boys tend to think it looks more masculine to jump in single, high jumps. Maybe. But it's easier to jump with a small bounce between the big bounces over the rope. It's also easier to jump with both feet together, rather than changing legs. Once you become used to the timing, tricks like jumping on one foot, or touching the ground when you jump, will seem simple.

Running in to the rope FRONT DOOR, is easier than BACK DOOR, because the rope is *falling toward you* and you don't have to jump as you enter. Watch and listen to the rhythm of the turning rope. Stand just far enough away so the rope doesn't hit you as it turns. As soon as it passes you on the way down, run to the spot where it hits the ground. You now have as much time as it takes for the rope to come around again to get yourself ready to jump over it. Start out with the rope turning slowly until you feel the rhythm. And stay relaxed. It's really not that hard. A little trial and error and you will be jumping with the best of them.

Running in BACK DOOR requires that you jump the rope *as you go in*. The rope is rising toward you and you must enter as soon as it passes you on the way *up*. But as soon as you get in, it will be coming down, and you must be prepared to jump over it quickly.

Once you are good enough to even *try* DOUBLE DUTCH, there's not much you can learn except by experience. The jumping motion is like running in place. At first, however, it's easier to jump DOUBLE DUTCH with both feet in a side-to-side motion, rather than alternating feet. For "Double Orange," or other games where the two ropes are turning *outward* you must jump higher, kicking your legs out and up to the sides, as the ropes are crossing under you and rising out.

It's actually easier to run in to "Double Orange," where the ropes are FRONT DOOR from either side. In "Double Dutch," you must run in BACK DOOR. But for all two-rope games, the best advice is to *watch one rope*. You'll go crazy watching both of them.

Rope health

A Physical Fitness Program*

Imagine for a moment that you are setting out to run a mile. (That might take a lot of imagination.) If you are like millions of other Americans, after a few minutes your chest will start heaving as your lungs gasp for air; your heart will pound wildly as it struggles to pump blood through your body; the blood will rush madly through your circulatory system. You'll be a wreck. And, what's more, it will take you quite some time to start feeling normal again. You will be experiencing what is known as *circulatory fatigue,* the result of a lack of

*The material in this chapter has been reviewed by Dr. Robert C. Darling, Professor Emeritus of Rehabilitation Medicine at Columbia Presbyterian Medical Center in New York and an author in the field of exercise physiology. He has found the information medically sound and the exercise programs medically safe.

cardiovascular fitness.

According to many of today's leading medical authorities on exercise, cardiovascular fitness (loosely speaking, the health of the heart and circulatory system, including the lungs) is the most important kind of "physical fitness" for the average man or woman. In fact, a program aimed at developing cardiovascular fitness is the official exercise program of both the United States Air Force and the Royal Canadian Air Force. And the key to it all is oxygen delivery.

The human body requires energy constantly. Even when you are fast asleep you need energy just to keep breathing. And the more strenuous the activity, the greater the demand in energy. The *circulatory fatigue* described above is the body's own energy crisis. To produce energy, the body *burns fuel*. The fuel is food, and the "burning agent" or flame is oxygen. But unless we are literally starving, this energy crisis isn't the result of a shortage of fuel—food. It comes from a shortage of flame—oxygen.

The body can store food. As we go through the day, we burn the necessary fuel for our immediate needs and store the rest as fat tissue. But the body can't store oxygen, which is why we must keep breathing, in and out, all our lives. The oxygen is carried in our blood—in the hemoglobin of the red blood cells. The food waits for the oxygen in every nook, cranny, and corner of our bodies. It waits to be burned to produce the energy required to keep our various muscles, organs, and spare parts functioning. But in many a body beautiful, the unseen means for delivering the oxygen— the lungs, heart, and blood vessels—have become run-down from disuse, or under-use. As a result, our demand for energy exceeds our capacity to produce it.

Think about that mile-running wreck again. Those heaving lungs are gasping for oxygen. That pounding heart is pumping oxygen And that rushing blood is delivering oxygen. Which, believe it or not, brings us to jump-rope.

The Training Effect

Jumping rope is one of many exercises which can build up the oxygen-delivery systems of your body and provide that all-important cardiovascular fitness. Athletes have long recognized this value of jumping rope as well as its additional role in developing hand-foot coordination, agility, and stamina. Cardiovascular fitness is achieved means of week-by-week programs of increasing difficulty. These programs, patterned on official Air Force regimens, take into account differences of age and sex. But they have a single, simple objective: to gradually condition your heart to accept a sustained rate of 130 to 150 beats per minute without fatigue. From this single good thing, many other good things follow.

According to an eminent medical authority on the physiology of exercise "a fundamental characteristic of the systems involved in exercise is that they adapt to meet the new condition of exercise. . . . The adaptations . . . occur at two levels. First, there are immediate changes during and after a bout of exercise. Second, there is the set of adaptive changes which permit the organism to improve function during later bouts of exercise. These latter may be called *training effects*"* (italics mine).

The "training effects" ascribed to my graded jump-rope exercise programs and to similar programs in jogging, running, swimming, cycling, and other activities are facts. They are not mere guesswork, but have been documented in various laboratories by medical researchers using modern techniques and equipment. Much of this research has been done by Dr. Kenneth Cooper of the United States Air Force.

*Robert C. Darling, M.D., *Physiological Basis of Rehabilitation Medicine* (Philadelphia: W. B. Saunders Co., 1971), p. 167.

While I will attempt to outline all of the training effects which occur throughout the oxygen-delivery system, three of them are most important and worthy of special emphasis. "[The] first and most striking of these is the increased volume and flow [of oxygen-containing blood] in the exercising muscles, as a result of . . . the opening of [blood vessels] which were previously closed." Blood distribution becomes more selective, for along with this increased flow to working muscles, including the heart, "circulation to other systems of the body is reduced,"* particularly to the liver and the kidneys. These two effects are known respectively as vascularization and vasoconstriction, and will be explained more fully in the section on the blood vessels.

But perhaps the most significant training effect of all is an increase in "cardiac output." This in simplest terms means the amount of blood the heart is able to pump, and how quickly and efficiently it is able to pump it.

Keeping in mind that oxygen delivery is the key, let's take a closer look at the "training effects" of a jump-rope exercise program.

The Lungs

Our oxygen-delivery system begins in the lungs. We breathe air containing 21 percent oxygen into our lungs. The oxygen attaches itself to the hemoglobin in our red blood cells. The

*Ibid., 177.

blood is pumped by the heart through the arteries to all the millions of cells in the body. In the cells, the oxygen "flame" ignites the food "fuel" to produce energy. The main by-product of this burning is carbon dioxide, which now replaces the oxygen in the blood and is carried back to the lungs through the veins. The carbon dioxide wastes are expelled from the lungs when we exhale, leaving the blood free to pick up more oxygen.

There are two factors which affect the amount of oxygen our lungs can process, and exercise produces training effects on both of them. The first deals with our mechanism for pulling air into the lungs—inhaling—and pushing waste materials out—exhaling. When you breathe, muscles in your chest cause your rib cage and diaphragm to expand. This creates a lowered pressure in your lung cavity, and air rushes into the lungs. Other chest muscles also create a contraction of the rib cage, which along with the natural elastic recoil of the lungs, forces carbon dioxide out as you exhale. Exercise will strengthen these muscles of respiration, resulting in a greater capacity to process oxygen.

The second factor affecting our lungs' part in oxygen delivery is known as their vital capacity. This is a simple measure not of the size of the lungs, but rather of their usable portion, and is based upon the amount of air exhaled in one deep breath. It has been established that the training effect of a conscientious exercise program results in a vital capacity of approximately 75 percent of total lung capacity. However, while "untrained"

lungs might equal this, during a bout of strenuous exercise "trained" lungs can process at least twice the amount of air per minute as untrained lungs—in the first case approximately twenty times the vital capacity per minute; in the latter case, less than ten.

The Blood Vessels

When we inhale, the air in our lungs is forced into millions of tiny air sacs called alveoli. These sacs are surrounded by blood, and it is here, through a process controlled by adjacent areas of high and low pressures, that the oxygen attaches itself to the hemoglobin in the red blood cells.

There are several training effects on the blood vessels. The first is to make them larger and more pliable, usually with an accompanying decrease in blood pressure. During exercise, the blood is forced through the vessels more rapidly and forcefully than usual. Soon the blood vessels adapt to this condition and reduce their resistance to blood flow.

The second, rather spectacular training effect is known as vascularization—an actual increase in the *number* of blood vessels. New networks of vessels open up to saturate the tissues of the involved muscles with oxygen and remove wastes more effectively. Most often, this process occurs not vessel by vessel but network by network—in leaps and bounds. Vascularization results in a decrease in muscular fatigue and an increase in

endurance. And, of course, there is an all-important increase in the oxygen supply to the heart tissue itelf.

As we have seen, vascularization is accompanied by vasoconstriction, or a cut-down of the blood supply to areas whose oxygen demands are not as great during exercise. The liver and the kidneys are the main areas involved. So the two "V's" combine to train the body to distribute its oxygen supply more selectively during periods of high energy demand.

The final training effect on the blood vessels is somewhat indirect. Strenuous physical activity helps the body's tissue metabolism—the process of changing food into tissue—particularly in breaking down fats, such as cholesterol. Cholesterol is found in the crust which forms inside hardened arteries. Exercise, which helps to break down these fats, thus helps to keep the arteries free of excess cholesterol.

The Muscles And the Heart

A jump-rope exercise program will strengthen some of your muscles and make all of them healthier. Conditioned muscle tissue becomes longer and leaner, bringing all of the tissue closer to the oxygen supply in the blood vessels. And besides, the blood vessels have increased in number.

The heavily involved muscles of the legs, arms, and shoulders will become stronger, and all of your muscles will improve their "tone."

There are also three significant training effects on the heart, the most important muscle of them all.

The first is, of course, increased "cardiac output." As I've said earlier, the single objective of the exercise programs, from which all other benefits flow, is to condition the heart to sustain a rate of 130 to 150 beats per minute without fatigue. The heart *can be trained* to pump more oxygen-filled blood more rapidly to the tissues, and more carbon-dioxide-filled blood back to the lungs. This is what is meant by "increased cardiac output."

The overall health of the heart tissue depends in large measure upon its own supply of blood vessels. As we noted before, the oxygen supply to the heart is significantly affected by vascularization. Heart tissue is more likely to remain healthy when the oxygen needs for its own energy requirements are comfortably met.

The final training effect on the heart is a reduced heart rate. The trained heart can beat more slowly because it can pump more blood with each stroke. Think of it this way — if you can cut your heart rate by 10 to 15 beats per minute, which is not uncommon, you will be saving it 15,000 to 20,000 beats per day! It will thank you for your thoughtfulness.

Bonus Benefits

In addition to the laboratory-proven cardiovascular training effects, there are several other interesting and significant side-effects of a jump-rope exercise program. These are a bit less scientific, but have been experienced by enough people to make the odds pretty good that they'll happen to you.

1. *Your digestion will improve*. Exercise conditions the muscles of the digestive tract, permitting it to move wastes more effectively. And conditioned people generally produce less stomach acid.

2. *You'll lose some weight, or not gain any*. As we've seen, exercise changes fat muscle to lean muscle. This can certainly help you take a few inches off your hips. Exercise also makes you burn excess calories before they settle in as fat tissue. Finally, exercising people generally crave a lot of fluids, which help to curb indulgent appetites.

3. *Your bust will have better support*. The arm and shoulder movements connected with jumping rope will build up your pectoral muscles, which support the breasts. Women, incidentally, particularly buxom ones, are advised to wear a firmly supportive bra when jumping rope.

4. *You'll have more energy*. The improved oxygen delivery system makes the normal energy demands of your body easier to meet. Exercise also *helps you to work off tension*. And if you're less tense, *you'll sleep better*.

Ready, Set, Go

In these exercise programs, jumping rope may be done to records, a metronome, or—if you're tuned

in—to the music of the spheres. Housewives have been known to organize jump-rope clubs which nicely combine physical conditioning and camaraderie.

The charts which follow are designed to build you up gradually. They differ somewhat according to your age and sex. The reasons behind the age differences should be fairly obvious, but I'd better protect myself from feminist assault. A woman's oxygen-processing capacity is usually smaller than a man's. This is due to her generally smaller physical size, as well as a smaller heart and lung capacity. Women also have less blood, which means less hemoglobin.

Now that you know all about the magnificent training effects of the programs, you might wonder why they can't be achieved by simply jumping five minutes a day from now to the millennium. According to the medical authorities "the exercise must be of sufficient intensity and duration to raise cardiac output to near-maximum. . . . The absolute level of the exercise must be related to the present capacity of the exercising individual and *must be progressively increased in intensity as the individual gains capacity from the exercise"* (italics mine).

Once you've built up to the highest level on your chart, you and your oxygen-delivery system will be in really splendid shape. Of course the first weeks are hardest, and of course you'll want to quit, and of course you shouldn't.

Ibid., p. 77.

There is one basic precaution which I can't emphasize too strongly. Before you begin an exercise program, *see your doctor*. This is particularly true if you're over 30 and haven't had a checkup within the last year. In any case, it is always wise to have a pre-exercise physical.

The charts have left you one important area for creative thinking. They tell you *how long* to jump—pretty continuously without a lot of resting. And *how fast* to jump—70 to 80 jumps per minute. But *how* you jump is up to you. To keep things interesting, I recommend putting together some routines of fancy footwork from the "Rope How" chapter. Just as an example, here's a typical routine which should take three or three and a half minutes to run through:

1. 10 DOUBLE HEEL HOPS
2. 10 DOUBLE TOE TAPS
3. 7 HEEL-TO-TOE-DOUBLE WHAMMYS (Steps 1–6)
4. 5 HEEL-TO-TOE CROSS-AS-YOU-GOS with right foot.
5. 5 HEEL-TO-TOE CROSS-AS-YOU-GOS with left foot.
6. 5 BACK-TO-BACK THINGUMACRACKS with right foot.
7. 5 BACK-TO-BACK THINGUMACRACKS with left foot.

You should always have a brief warm-up period before you begin the day's exercise. Stretching exercises, described in any calisthenics book, are excellent. A few sit-ups and push-ups can't hurt. The warm-up period is also good for practicing a new step. Don't try to learn a new one during the timed exercising. You're almost certain to keep messing it up and stopping, so you just won't be working your heart hard enough.

It's also a good idea to take a brief cool-down period after the timed jumping. This can be as simple as five minutes of walking around slowly. After rope jumping, a lot of blood will be in your legs. It takes a few minutes to get this blood back into circulation, and if you stand still or sit down immediately, you just might faint.

Take a good look at yourself, summon up your will power, see your doctor, cut down your clothesline—and get healthy.

Graded Programs

Here are the week-by-week programs for men and women in various age categories. Remember that the rate of skipping should be from 70 to 80 jumps per minute. Though you should certainly stop jumping if you begin to feel light-headed, dizzy, or nauseated, or experience tightness or pains in the chest, the programs are designed for fairly continuous activity. If you keep stopping to rest, your heart will not build up to the desired level of stress. However, if the charts call for a faster rate of progress than you can manage, don't worry. And don't give up. Just stay at a comfortable level until you can go on.

UNDER 30			
WEEK	WOMEN'S TIME	MEN'S TIME	DAYS PER WEEK
1	2 min	3 min	5
2	4 min	5 min	5
3	5 min	7 min	5
4	7 min	8 min	5
5	8 min	10 min	5
6	10 min	12 min	5
7	12 min	13 min	5
8	13 min	15 min	5
9	14 min	16 min	5
10	15 min (or 10 min in A.M. plus 5 min in P.M.)	17 min (or 10 min in A.M. plus 10 min in P.M.)	5

AGE 30–39			
WEEK	WOMEN'S TIME	MEN'S TIME	DAYS PER WEEK
1	2 min	3 min	5
2	3 min	4 min	5
3	4 min	5 min	5
4	5 min	6 min	5
5	7 min	8 min	5
6	8 min	10 min	5
7	10 min	12 min	5
8	11 min	13 min	5
9	12 min	14 min	5
10	13 min	15 min	5
11	14 min	16 min	5
12	15 min (or 10 min in A.M. plus 5 min in P.M.)	17 min (or 10 min in A.M. plus 10 min in P.M.)	

AGE 40–49			
WEEK	WOMEN'S TIME	MEN'S TIME	DAYS PER WEEK
1	2 min	3 min	5
2	3 min	4 min	5
3	4 min	5 min	5
4	5 min	6 min	5
5	6 min	7 min	5
6	7 min	8 min	5
7	8 min	10 min	5
8	9 min	11 min	5
9	10 min	12 min	5
10	11 min	13 min	5
11	12 min	14 min	5
12	13 min	15 min	5
13	14 min	16 min	5
14	15 min (or 10 min in A.M. plus 5 min in P.M.)	17 min (or 10 min in A.M. plus 5 min in P.M.)	5

AGE 50–59			
WEEK	WOMEN'S TIME	MEN'S TIME	DAYS PER WEEK
1	1 min	2 min	5
2	2 min	3 min	5
3	3 min	4 min	5
4	4 min	5 min	5
5	5 min	6 min	5
6	5 min	7 min	5
7	6 min	8 min	5
8	7 min	9 min	5
9	8 min	10 min	5
10	9 min	11 min	5
11	10 min	12 min	5
12	11 min	13 min	5
13	12 min	14 min	5
14	13 min	15 min	5
15	14 min	16 min	5
16	15 min (or 10 min. in A.M. plus 5 min in P.M.)	17 min (or 10 min in A.M. plus 10 min in P.M.)	5

Not recommended for those over 60

"Chinese Jump Rope"

Rope play

Jump-Rope Games

For hundreds of years kids all over the world have entertained themselves with little more equipment than a rope or two and some imagination. They have created games and stunts to amuse themselves or to compete with their playmates.

Many of these games use no rhymes, while others have very specific ones. Still others use any rhyme at all. And kids in some places think of some rhymes as games, and vice versa. So if you don't find what you're looking for in this section, you may come across it later on.

It's important to remember that general conditions or house rules may be placed on many of the games to make them more challenging; for example, declaring that players must run in BACK DOOR, or enter ON TIME, or run around the ENDERS at a certain time. Penalties for missing a jump can vary as well, from taking an end to going to the back of the line, to being eliminated from the rest of the game.

Try the glossary if the terms confuse you. And if you are a BLACK SHEEP and have trouble jumping or running in, try the tips on technique in the "Rope How" chapter.

Simple Games

Solo Stunts

There are many ways of jumping all alone with your own rope. These games are fun and also good practice for jumping in groups. With or without your favorite rhymes, try some of these.

One-Handed: Put a small weight on one end of the rope (a tennis ball works well), spin it with one hand, and jump over it.

Jump Turn: Turn around while jumping.

In And Out: Alternate jumps with your feet close together and then spread apart.

Heel-Heel: Jump with a hopping bounce, putting your left heel forward on one jump, and your right heel forward on the next.

Hopsies: (See page 29.)

Leg Swing: Hop on one foot, swinging the other foot back and forth.

Legs Crossed: Jump on both feet, but with your legs crossed at the ankles.

Rock: Put one foot in front of the other. Jump on your front foot, then your back foot, rocking back and forth.

Toe Tap: Hop on one leg, keeping the other leg straight and tapping your toe in front or in back.

Tap Dance: Hop on one foot, doing a brush and a tap with the other foot between jumps.

Crossie: (See page 26.)

Double-Skip: Turn the rope fast enough, and jump high enough, so that the rope goes under your feet twice on each jump. This is great practice for a game of ''Bumps.'' Bend slightly at the waist, keep your legs straight and point your toes.

Ball Bouncing: This is a tricky stunt which comes from Nebraska. Frankly, I've never seen it done. Hold a ball in one hand, along with one end of the rope. Drop the ball so the rope turns under your feet and the bouncing ball simultaneously.

Games for Two Or Three

Here are games for a few players. Remember that one end of the rope can be tied to a tree or pole when you can't round up another ender.

Two-On-One: This is my own name for an easy game for two jumpers. The players stand side by side facing in the same direction. One turns the rope with the right hand, the other with the left.

Jump together. You can make this game a bit harder by turning the rope backward over your heads, or by facing in opposite directions.

Visiting: This nineteenth-century game and the next one, "Best Friend," are games in which one player turns the rope. In "Visiting" one jumper turns the rope and another jumps in to "visit," facing the turner. They jump together for a while. Then the visitor jumps out without the rope stopping, making room for another visitor to enter.

"Two-On-Two"

Best Friend: This game uses one of many "Call In" rhymes, in which the jumper calls out the name of another player to join or follow in the rope. There are several rhymes listed later in the book, but the one used in "Best Friend" is one of the oldest.

> I call in my very best friend
> And that is ___ _____. [name another player]
> One, two, three!

On "three!" the "best friend" jumps in facing the turner, as in "Visiting." Now the two jump to any other rhyme they like. Then the friend jumps out so another "best friend" can be invited in. The turner can invite more than one friend in at a time, but any more than two [one in front and one in back] is inviting disaster.

Two-On-Two: This name is my own, but the game has been played for over a century. Two players turn one long rope while a third player runs in turning and jumping a short rope. The two ropes can be jumped together or in succession. Both may be turned FRONT DOOR, both BACK DOOR, or to really impress the onlookers, turn one rope FRONT and the other BACK DOOR.

Calling In: This CALL-IN game is really more fun with several players, but the minimum requirements are four people and one tree. One player runs in. On the second jump, she calls someone's name, and that player runs in to be with the caller for the third jump. After jumping the third jump together, the caller runs out on the opposite side, and the friend in turn calls in someone else on her second jump, and so on.

Simple Group Games

Most of these games are quite old, and fun for beginners.

The Ladder: This game dates from the nineteenth century. The player runs in to jump, first on one foot and then on the other, with a stepping motion like climbing a ladder or a flight of stairs.

Winding The Clock: Another early game in which the jumper counts to twelve, turning around on each jump.

Baking Bread: W.H. Babcock writing in *Lippincott's Magazine* in 1886 describes this game as played by girls in Washington, D.C.: "The performer holds in one hand a stone [representing a loaf of bread, I suppose] while she jumps three times. Then she puts the stone down and jumps three times without it. This alternation continues till she comes in contact with the rope and has to change places with one of the turners." In a slight variation, the rope is spun over the jumper's head three times [OVER THE WATER] as the stone is put down, then turned normally again when it is picked up. See also the action games "Baby in the Cradle," and "One way, Two way."

Follow The Leader: In jump-rope, a simple game of follow-the-leader can become as difficult as the skill of the players permits. Generally, when the leader misses, the next person in line takes over.

Chase The Fox: A time-honored follow-the -leader type of game in which the leader is the "fox" and the other players "geese." The fox runs through the rope FRONT DOOR without jumping and the geese follow. Then the geese follow the fox through BACK DOOR without jumping. Continuing to run in FRONT DOOR, then BACK DOOR, fox and geese proceed to jump once, then twice and so on, until someone misses. The first to do so takes an end, and the turner becomes one of the geese. This game is also known as "Fox and Geese," "Fox-a-Go-Geese," "Running Through the Moon," and "Changing Partners." In some versions, a player who misses is eliminated.

Running Through School: The players run through a turning rope without jumping as the others shout "Kindergarten." They jump once for "First grade" twice for "Second grade," etc., up to twelve. For college years, one through four, the players must enter BACK DOOR. Naturally, you fail the grade if you miss, and must try again on your next turn, keeping your nose in the books until you "graduate." Also called "School."

Cut The Moon: This game may be played with a turning rope or a swaying [BLUEBELLS] rope. The players run in at the end of the rope, touch the turner's hand, jump once, and run out on the same side as they ran in. On each round the number of jumps increases, up to twelve, as the player moves from one end of the rope to the other [UP THE LADDER]. On the final turn, you must touch one ender's hand, jump twelve times to the other end without missing, and touch the other ender's hand.

Ten And A Journey: This is an interesting Scottish follow-the-leader game. The leader jumps ten times, says a rhyme of her choice, jumps out and takes a "journey" around the playground, gym or street. The others imitate her exactly, jumping ten times, repeating her rhyme, and following her journey back to the rope. The length of the journey will depend on the number of players, since each player must return to take her next turn ON TIME.

High Water, Low Water: The rope is held stationary a few inches above the ground as the players jump over it. It is raised slightly each time, either a definite number of times—such as the age of the jumper—or indefinitely, until everyone is eliminated. This game was played in the 1880's as "Pile of Bricks," where each elevation of the rope was a "brick," and is also known as "Building House," and "Building Up the Castle." For rhymes jumped to a rising rope see "Fudge, fudge, call the judge," and "When it rains, the Mississippi."

Baby's Cradle: The rope sways back and forth at the same height (BLUEBELLS) as the players jump from side to side or front to back, continuing until they miss. In "Rocking the Cradle," the rope sways three times, then turns three times until the jumper misses.

Snake: The rope is wriggled side to side on the ground as the players try to jump over it without being "bitten." A description of this game from the 1920's claims that the rope was undulated so sharply that the players, if caught, would go sprawling to the ground unless one of the turner's graciously released his end.

Tidal Waves: A combination of "Snake" and "High Water, Low Water." The rope is swayed from side to side and gradually raised higher and higher until all the players are eliminated. This version is also known as "Snakes and Ladders."

Cut The Cheese: As in "Snake," and "Tidal Waves," the rope is wriggled sharply, but with an up-and-down, rather than side-to-side motion.

Sweet Stuff Shop: One of the few games in which turning can be fun. Each of the enders secretly chooses some kind of candy or other "sweet stuff." The players run through, shouting guesses at the enders' secret sweets. If they guess wrong, they go to the end of the line. But when they guess right, they take the place of the ender whose secret has been revealed and choose a secret of their own. The game is also played with secret colors or produce, called respectively "Colors" and "Fruit Store."

Jump The Shot: A weight, such as a rubber ball, is attached to the end of a rope. The players stand in a circle around the turner, who swings the ball around a few inches from the ground. The players must "jump the shot" as it comes to them, dropping out of the circle if hit by the rope or the ball. This game is also known as "The Whip" and, in France, as "The Serpent." In the version known as "Round Rope Heights," the turner can swing the rope higher and faster as players are eliminated, varying his movements in an attempt to catch those remaining.

Multijumpers

There are several jump-rope games which have two or more people in the rope at the same time. In addition to the six games in this group and the

CALL IN games and rhymes, there are other good verses for multijumping in the section on rhymes.

Marriage By The Knife: This was one of the games described by W.H. Babcock in 1886. He called it "the most interesting game of the rope," and it does have a fascinating ritual-like quality. The rhyme, like many of the earliest verses used for jump-rope, derives from an English singing game—in this case "Poor Mary Sits A-Weeping." Two players run in and jump side by side as the others chant:

> By the Holy and religerally law,
> I marry this Indian to this squaw;
> By the point of my jack-knife,
> I pronounce you man and wife.
>
> Now you're married, you must be good,
> And make your husband chop the wood.
> You must be kind, you must be true,
> And kiss the bride and she'll kiss you.
>
> Sober live and sober proceed,
> And so bring up your Indian breed.
> You may go, the wedding's done;
> Count your children one by one.
> 1,2,3,4, etc. [until jumpers miss].

Grinding Coffee: This game is named for an old-fashioned coffee grinder in which the grinding wheel revolves around a central core. One jumper jumps in place, and a second player jumps around her in a tight circle.

Begging: The first player, the "beggar," is joined by a second player and they jump side by side. While still jumping, they change places (PASS THE BAKER). As they pass, the beggar says, "Give me some bread and butter." The other answers, "Try my next door neighbor," and runs out.

Now another player runs in, jumps side by side and changes places. The beggar asks again for some bread and butter. This is repeated until the beggar misses and another player becomes the beggar.

Kings And Queens: For this rhyme game there are two lines of players—the "Kings" and the "Queens." One line stands at each end of the rope, but both lines can enter FRONT DOOR, both BACK DOOR, or from opposite sides. A King enters on "Kings;" a Queen on "Queens." At "how do you do" they shake hands and change places, running out at "One, two, three."

> Kings and Queens
> And partners two,
> All dressed up in royal blue.
>
> One, two, how do you do?
>
> I do very well
> With a house to myself,
> A key to my door
> And a rug on the floor.
>
> One, two, three.

"Begging"

Ten Little Indians: This well-known children's song is jumped to in Nebraska and, I would guess, in other places as well. It works best when there are ten jumpers who enter one at a time and run out in the same order.

> 1 little, 2 little, 3 little Indians,
> 4 little, 5 little, 6 little Indians,
> 7 little, 8 little, 9 little Indians,
> 10 little Indian boys.
>
> 10 little, 9 little, 8 little Indians,
> 7 little, 6 little, 5 little Indians,
> 4 little, 3 little, 2 little Indians,
> 1 little Indian boy.

All In Together: This is a game form of one of the oldest jump-rope rhymes which has been traced to ancient Rome and Roman Britain. There are probably as many American forms today as there are states, and several of these will appear later in various rhyme groups.

In this game version, all jumpers enter together, which can become a madhouse with lots of players. Those who survive the running in continue to jump and run out individually on their birthday month. The last player in the rope gets HOT PEPPER for some predetermined number of jumps.

If you trip going in or in the middle of the rhyme, you are eliminated. But if you are the one to get PEPPER, you become a turner if you miss. Nevertheless, I would suspect that this game is most appealing to jumpers born in December.

> All in together,
> This fine weather.
> Trip stays out,
> And the last pepper.
> January, February, March, etc.

Super Games

Action Games, Stunts, And Special Games

These games call for various pantomimes or actions from the jumpers. Many action rhymes are considered games in their own right, although they have been included in the rhymes section of the book. For example, there are many rhymes which call for the same action as "Banana Split." The special games "Chinese Jump-Rope," "Report Card," and "Patricia, Patricia" are all rare, but terrific!

Banana Split: In this game the jumper must catch the rope between the legs on the word "split(s)" at the end of each line.

> Went to the drugstore to get a banana split.
> One banana, two banana, three banana
> splits!

Mississippi: There are three ways of playing "Mississippi."

In the first two variations, the jumper spells the

c. Skim the milk turning on each jump.
d. Skim the milk jumping with feet crossed.
e. Skim the milk hopping on one foot.
f. Skim the milk hopping and turning.
g. Skim the milk bouncing a ball.
h. Skim the milk tossing a ball.
i. Skim the milk alternately tossing and
    bouncing a ball.

Chinese Jump-Rope: While this game is not very common in the United States, it has been played in Delaware and Massachusetts. A simpler form called "Indian Jumping" is played in Philadelphia. Forms of the game are, however, very popular in Greece, India, Afghanistan, Turkey, Argentina, and Scotland, where it is variously known as "Chinese Ropes," "American Ropes," and "Elastications."

The American version, "Chinese Jump-Rope," uses an 8-to-10-foot circle of either rope or tied-together rubber bands. The ENDERS step into the circle and move as far apart as necessary to make the ropes or bands taut around their ankles, forming two parallel lines about one foot apart.

1. Stand sideways to the long circle, put one foot in the middle, touch the ground with your toes and remove your foot, without touching the ropes. Place your foot under the closest rope and carry it over the far rope, touch your toe on the far side of the circle and bring your foot back. Repeat five times. Now move to the other side of the circle and repeat all of Step 1 five times from the other side.

(See photographs on pages 54, 68, 130, 138.)

2. The rope is now raised to your knee level. Stand in the center of the circle, facing one of the enders. Jump and place your legs outside the circle, [without touching the ropes]then jump back in again. Repeat five times facing one ender and five times facing the other.

3. The rope is arranged so that one side is about six inches higher than the other. Face the circle and jump into it over the low rope, then out over the high rope. Now jump *backward* over the high rope into the circle, and out over the low rope. Repeat five times.

4. The rope is placed at ankle level, as in Step 1. Perform the actions of Step 1 with your hands, instead of your feet.

5. Rope at knee level, as in Step 2. Perform Step 2 with *hands and feet* touching the ground outside the circle when you jump.

6. Rope in position for Step 3. Jump forward and backward over the rope with hands touching the ground when you jump.

If you miss on any step, you must start again!

American Ropes: This is the Scottish version of "Chinese Jump-Rope. ''The ENDERS form the circle of rubber bands in the same way, starting around the ankles.

1. Stand sideways to the circle, put a foot in the middle, take it out.

2. Carry the near band over the other with the point of your toe and bring it back. Repeat ten times with one foot.

3. Change sides and repeat Steps 1–2 ten times with the other foot.

"Chinese Jump Rope"

4. Jump into the circle with both feet, then out again. Repeat ten times. Jump, using both feet to carry the near band over the far band and back. Repeat 10 times.

5. Repeat these same moves with the bands at knee level, waist level ("Waisties") and neck level ("Headies").

I doubt that any player can really execute Steps 2 and 4 at "Headies." However, Step 1 can be done by many players, and shorter performers have been known to enter the circle by means of a cartwheel or handstand!

Indian Jumping: In South Philadelphia, players do "Indian Jumping" to rhymes of their choice. The movements are those of Steps 1–2 of "American Ropes." Alternate the moves rapidly until you miss.

Report Card: Two of the most fascinating examples of jump-rope folklore are the story games "Report Card and "Patricia, Patricia." Both come from North Carolina.

In "Report Card," the jumper moves up and down the rope between the "Teacher" ender and the "Mother" ender. All three act out their roles in the drama, and the rhythm and movement of the rope changes with the plot, which is a wonderful commentary on breakfast-hour confusion in busy households.

The jumper starts at "Mother's" end of the rope, which sways smoothly [BLUEBELLS].

Jumper: Good-by, Mama.
1st End: Good-by, darlin'.
      [BLUEBELLS to other end of rope]
Jumper: Good morning, Teacher.
      [full, sharp turning]
2nd End: Good morning, Patsy.
      Where's your report card?
Jumper: I left it at home.
2nd End: Go right home and get it!
      [HOT PEAS to "Mother's" end]
Jumper: Mama, Mama!
      Where's my report card?
      [slow, hesitant turns, with pauses for effect]
1st End: I'm not sure,
      But I think
      Baby chewed it up and Mama threw it in the fire. [slow, sulking return to "Teacher."]
Jumper: Teacher,
      Baby chewed it up and Mama threw it in the fire. [fast, sharp turning]
2nd End: Which do you want,
      A whipping or a licking?
      [jumper chooses one and jumps till she misses or tires]

In some versions, the choice is a "whipping" or "a scolding." In either case, "a whipping" is HOT PEAS and "a licking" or "a scolding" is high waters 1.

Patricia, Patricia: This short drama portrays a typical middle-class evening in a Southern home of the early 1900's. It also mocks the social custom, described in *Gone With the Wind,* that a marriage proposal should not be accepted until the third offer.

[slow, BLUEBELLS rope]
One evening,
When I was playing the piano
And Ma was sewing a green strip
And Pa was reading the paper,
Came a great knock at the door.

[Slow, high turning]
"Patricia, Patricia,
Go to that door."
"Yes, sir. Yes, sir."
But I didn't do it.

"Patricia, Patricia,
Go to that door."
'Yes, sir. Yes, sir."
But I didn't do it.

"Patricia, Patricia,
Go to that door."
"Yes, sir. Yes, sir."
I did it that time.

[slow, BLUEBELLS rope]
Big, tall skinny man
Standing at the door.
I asked him in.

[fast, HIGH WATERS turning]
He talked politics and Rolly-tics,*
And Rolly-tics and politics,
And politics and Rolly-tics,
        [repeat until jumper tires and
        decides to go "upstairs"—to
        the other end of the rope]
Till I got tired and
Went upstairs to bed.

[slow, BLUEBELLS rope]
Next night,
When I was playing the piano
And Ma was sewing a green strip
And Pa was reading the paper,
Came a great knock at the door.

        [repeat the three verses getting
        Patricia to the door with slow, high
        turning; then, BLUEBELLS rope]
Big fat man; same tall, skinny man,
Standing at the door.
Big, fat man said:
        [slow, high turning]
"Patricia, Patricia,
Will you marry me?"
"Yes, sir, Yes, sir."
But I didn't do it.

---

*A folk term coined for the political "Rhamkatte Roaster" column in the Raleigh, North Carolina, *News and Observer.*

"Patricia, Patricia,
Will you marry me?"
"Yes, sir. Yes, sir."
But I didn't do it.

"Patricia, Patricia,
Will you marry me?"
"Yes, sir. Yes, sir."
I did it that time!

Speed, Timing, And Double-Rope Games

These games are really tricky, particularly "Chase," "Bumps," and the fiercely competitive "Partners Double-Dutch."

In addition to the game listed, there are countless rhymes which call for a gradual increase in speed, such as "One to make ready," "Baker, Baker," and the notorious "Mabel, Mabel." These will be found later in the section on hot rhymes, although, like some action rhymes, they are generally regarded as games by those who play them.

Keep The Kettle Boiling: This is the simplest example of an ON TIME game, in which a steady rhythm is maintained by the jumpers as they run in to the rope. If you hesitate, or enter and miss, you must take an end.

In Maine, the chant is:

Keep the kettle boiling,
1,2,3, etc.

Utah jumpers repeat the lines:

Keep the pot a-boiling,
Be on time.

As a perfect example of the way jump-rope rhymes spread geographically, it's likely that the Utah version originated in New England, which was the American arrival point for most of the Anglo-Saxon rhymes using the English ballad form of "a-knocking," "a-weeping," and "a-boiling." An English version of this game requires the player in at "December" to do PEPPER as the calendar is repeated. Again, tripping takes its toll.

Five, ten, fifteen, twenty,
Nobody leaves the jump-rope empty.
If they do, they shall suffer,
Take an end and be a duffer.
January, February, etc.

Stampede: This ON TIME game and the next three are all played with skill and enthusiasm by kids in Harlem today. I was pleased to discover that the preoccupation with the sights of London and France of my younger years has not been entirely lost.

Stampede!
Follow me
To the bottom of the sea.

While you're there,
Wash your hair
In your dirty underwear.

I see London,
I see France,
I see ———'s underpants.

Not too big,
Not too small,
Just the size of a cannonball.

Contest: Another popular ON TIME game. The "if possible" is arbitrary, and may be dropped in more competitive jump-rope circles.

Contest!
On time
If possible.
Got the A and the B,
C and the D,
E and the F,/etc.

Five, Four, Three, Twenty-One: This is an elimination ON TIME game, which gets trickier as players drop out. On the first line, "Five, four three, twenty-one," each player must run through the rope by entering FRONT DOOR, exiting BACK DOOR, and running around the ender back into place. If you hesitate or miss, you're out. The first line is repeated until all the remaining players, even those who have already made it, run through without a miss. In other words, all the remaining players must successfully run through one line before they can move on to the next line of the

rhyme. The elimination continues until, finally, the few remaining players must run through, without a rest-beat, to "One, one, one, one, etc." [Earlier lines all have a rest-beat between jumpers.]
Jump beats are underlined.

Five, four, three, twenty-one.
Four, three, twenty-one.
Three, twenty-one.
Twenty-one.
One [and one and one, etc.]

Chase: This exciting game is for four jumpers, though it can be played by more. The repeated chant is simple.

I said-a Chase
On
The
Third!
I said-a Chase
etc.

Players enter FRONT DOOR, ON TIME, on the accented words and jump once. You exit *on the same side* while the first player after you enters, run around the ender while the second player after you enters, and run in BACK DOOR *with* the third player after you. This crucial move is the "chase on the third." You continue by running out again on the back-door side, running around the *other* ender, and reentering with your "third." The diagram may help.

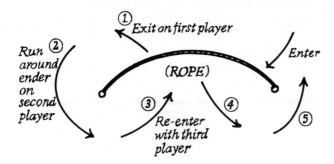

① Exit on first player

② Run around ender on second player

Enter

(ROPE)

③ Re-enter with third player

④

⑤

Bumps: One of the most popular Scottish jump-rope games, "Bumps" seems a likely candidate for American import. It uses Bump rhymes, one of which is given here. Others can be found on p.00.

The object is to jump to rhymes with "bump words," where the rope passes under the player twice on one jump. This, of course, requires that the player jump higher than usual, and that the ENDERS turn faster than usual. Try bending at the waist, keeping your legs straight and your toes pointed.

There are two ways for the jumper to increase the number of bumps. The first is to call CONTINUES! on the last regular bump. The enders must then turn additional bumps until the jumper misses. The more interesting way requires jumping through the rhyme several times, and increasing the number of bumps on the "bump-words" each

time. You begin with "Onesers," then two bumps on each bump-word for "Twosers," and continue up to "Sixsers." From there, you can start counting backward down to "Onesers" again.

Here is one bump rhyme. The "bump-words" are underlined.

> Ali Baba and the Forty <u>Thieves</u>
> Went to school with dirty <u>knees</u>.
> The teacher said, "Stand at <u>ease!</u>"
> Ali Baba and the Forty <u>Thieves</u>.

Irish: The simplest of the double-rope games is called "Irish" in New York, "French Jump-Rope" in some other parts of the country, and "German Ropes" in Great Britain.

Only one rope is turned. The other is stretched on the ground and may be kept taut by the feet of the turners. Actually, a chalk line would serve as well, and is used in many locales. The jumper of "Irish" must step over the line or stationary rope on each jump. If you fail to cross the line, touch it, or miss, you're out. Any rhyme can be used.

Over The Garden Wall: This is a DOUBLE DUTCH game which eliminates the problem of running in to the two-rope maze. The rhyme begins with a swaying rope, as in the game "Baby's Cradle." The player jumps this rope while *holding* the second rope which is stretched between the ENDERS. On the word "Over" in the last line, the player releases the rope in hand and the ENDERS turn both ropes DOUBLE DUTCH. The jumper continues until he misses.

Over the garden wall,
I let the baby fall.
My mother came out
And gave me a clout,
Over the garden wall.

Double Dutch; This ultimate test of the jumper's skill has been played since the 1890's. In those days, girls wore their dresses at ankle length, and as some old-timers have recollected, "It wasn't easy. You had to be good at Double Dutch, otherwise you would get a clout in the ear."*

DOUBLE DUTCH turning takes some practice, too. The ropes are turned in an eggbeater pattern, inward for DOUBLE DUTCH and outward for the more difficult DOUBLE ORANGE, DOUBLE IRISH, or SCOTCH.

Turners should hold one rope slightly higher than the other. Keep the high rope still and out to the side. Start turning the lower rope, then add the higher rope.

The jumper must skip one, then the other, in rapid succession with a running-in-place motion. Rhymes are used occasionally, such as the simple

Two, four, six-eight, ten,
Two, four, six-eight, twenty,
etc.

But as often as not, total concentration is required to suvive, let alone recite poetry!

---

*Brian Sutton-Smith, *The Folkgames of Children* (Austin: University of Texas Press, 1972).

Partners Double Dutch: If anything separates the WHITE SHEEP from the BLACK SHEEP, this is it. In "Partners" there are two teams with two jumpers per team. Each team turns for the other. Since a KISS (the two ropes touching) doesn't count against the jumper, it is extremely difficult to use turning strategy against your opponents. The players I watched were most honorable on this point.

Each player gets three turns, and the points are counted by tens (the syncopated counting rhythm used by New York players is fascinating and tricky). The team's six attempts are added cumulatively toward a total team score.

The game begins with a kind of pychological and physical preparation. The first jumper runs in and jumps while repeating the number "10" until her partner signals that she is ready to begin the actual scoring. On this signal, the warm-up jumper runs out as the first "scoring" jumper runs in, continuing the count with "20, 30, 40 . ..." by tens until she misses. At "100" the counting becomes syncopated, using "2, 3, 4," as shorthand for 20, 30, 40." The syncopated counting has no "9" for "ninety" but only 1–10,2,3,4,5,6,7,8; 2–10,2,3,4,5,6,7,8, etc. If, for example, you miss on "3–10,2,3,4," your score translates as 340. The other member of your team now begins with "5,6,7,8; 4–10,2,3,4,5,6,7,8," etc.

There is only one exception to this pattern. On one of your turns, you have the right to call "CONTINUATION!" when you miss. This requires

"A Kiss"

"Double Dutch"

the turning team to continue turning STRAIGHT ROPE until you miss again. The counting continues, however, as if there were no miss. The turning will be hot, but the extra points are added to your score, and they are easier than DOUBLE DUTCH points.

You can also make CONTINUATION a bit more difficult by requiring that the counting start over again from where your partner left off, and the continuation points only count if you exceed the DOUBLE DUTCH score you just missed on.

Whatever the local rules, PARTNERS offers the fastest track in town.

Rope rhymes

Jump-Rope Verses

Jump-rope rhymes are living language. As a rhyme travels from 1574 to 1974, England to New England, or Springfield, Illinois, to Springfield, Masaachusetts, or Long Island to Staten Island, subtle changes or bold revisions sneak in. The effects of time and geography can be seen and heard.

"All in Together," probably the oldest of the rhymes used for jump-rope, had its origins in Roman Britain. "Pan, Pan, Pan," a French rhyme from the sixteenth century, has been traced to the grotesque humor of Rabelais' *Gargantua and Pentagruel*.

These rhymes have endured; others come and go with the changing times, social conditions, and current events. Children of the Depression jumped to a rhyme which echoed household fears picked up from their anxious parents:

> *W.P.A.*
> *W.P.A.*
> *You're let out,*
> *Go get your pay.*

No more. To today's children the W.P.A. must sound like another radical terrorist organization.

But the many rhymes which have survived have picked up regional accents and dialects of their new homes. The old rhymes have borne offspring which resemble them, but often have mother's eyes, father's nose, and grandma's false teeth. Certainly they have lives of their own. A descendant of an old family like "All in Together" may be regarded as a counting rhyme in one community, but as an elimination or action rhyme in others.

For these reasons, a given rhyme might show up in several of the groups below, appearing in slightly different forms and serving different jump-rope functions. Of the many rhymes which have developed only slight regional variations, I have selected the variants which please me most, for totally subjective reasons.

As you amble through this garden of children's verses, however, keep in mind the words of another sometime jump-ropologist:

"There is, in all the ingenious boxes of the printers, no way to express in cold print the vigor, the vehemence of that rhythm, the effective use of pause, of which those little voices are capable."*

Four Classics

These four rhymes are among the most popular in the country and, in the case of "Teddy Bear," in the world.

For the budding folklorists and intellectually curious among you, they are given in all the significant variants I have run across.

Teddy Bear, Teddy Bear

More than any other, this rhyme transcends national, religious, and ethnic boundaries. The venerable bear is known in most of the United States, and has been spotted in South Africa, Luxembourg, Ecuador, and the Echigo Province of Japan where he is considered an old resident. These sightings seem to disprove the theory that the first President Roosevelt inspired the verse.

Whether known as Teddy Bear, Buster Brown, Ladybug, Butterfly, Spanish dancer, or Lady Lady, this action rhyme calls for a series of tricks while jumping.

Teddy Bear, Teddy Bear, turn around
Teddy Bear, Teddy Bear, touch the ground
Teddy Bear, Teddy Bear, shine your shoe
Teddy Bear, Teddy Bear, that will do
Teddy Bear, Teddy Bear, go upstairs
Teddy Bear, Teddy Bear, say your prayers
Teddy Bear, Teddy Bear, turn out the light
Teddy Bear, Teddy Bear, say goodnight
Teddy Bear, hop on one foot, one foot
Teddy Bear, hop on two feet, two feet
Teddy Bear, hop on three feet, three feet
Teddy Bear, hop right out

(New York)

---

*Edwin H. Adams, *Jump-Rope Rhymes* (Seattle: The Silver Quoin Press, 1947).

Teddy Bear, Teddy Bear, turn around
Teddy Bear, Teddy Bear, touch the ground
Teddy Bear, Teddy Bear, read the news
Teddy Bear, Teddy Bear, shine your shoes
Teddy Bear, Teddy Bear, go up the stairs
Teddy Bear, Teddy Bear, forget your cares
Teddy Bear, Teddy Bear, turn out the light
Teddy Bear, Teddy Bear, say goodnight

(Alabama)

Teddy Bear, Teddy Bear, turn all around
Teddy Bear, Teddy Bear, touch the ground
Teddy Bear, Teddy Bear, show your shoes
Teddy Bear, Teddy Bear, read the news
Teddy Bear, Teddy Bear, go upstairs
Teddy Bear, Teddy Bear, say your prayers
Teddy Bear, Teddy Bear, blow out the light
Teddy Bear, Teddy Bear, say goodnight
G-O-O-D-N-I-G-H-T

(Chicago)

Teddy Bear, Teddy Bear, turn all around
Teddy Bear, Teddy Bear, touch the ground
Teddy Bear, Teddy Bear, shine your shoe
Teddy Bear, Teddy Bear, how old are you?
1,2,3, etc.

(Delaware)

Teddy Bear, Teddy Bear, turn around
Teddy Bear, Teddy Bear, touch the ground
Teddy Bear, Teddy Bear, play some tricks
Teddy Bear, Teddy Bear, don't use sticks

(Maine)

Teddy Bear, Teddy Bear, turn around
Teddy Bear, Teddy Bear, touch the ground
Teddy Bear, Teddy Bear, show your shoe
Teddy Bear, Teddy Bear, now scud-doo [jumper
     runs out]
Teddy Bear, Teddy Bear, go upstairs
Teddy Bear, Teddy Bear, say your prayers
Teddy Bear, Teddy Bear, turn off the light
Teddy Bear, Teddy Bear, now goodnight
Teddy Bear, Teddy Bear, go to school
Teddy Bear, Teddy Bear, sit on the stool
Teddy Bear, Teddy Bear, read a book
Teddy Bear, Teddy Bear, spell goodnight
G-O-O-D-N-I-G-H-T

(Michigan)

Teddy Bear, Teddy Bear, turn around
Teddy Bear, Teddy Bear, touch the ground
Teddy Bear, Teddy Bear, tie your shoe
Teddy Bear, Teddy Bear, you'd better skidoo
Teddy Bear, Teddy Bear, go upstairs
Teddy Bear, Teddy Bear, say your prayers
Teddy Bear, Teddy Bear, switch off the light
Teddy Bear, Teddy Bear, say good night

(Nebraska)

Teddy Bear, Teddy Bear, turn around
Teddy Bear, Teddy Bear, touch the ground
Teddy Bear, Teddy Bear, buckle your shoe
Teddy Bear, Teddy Bear, that will do [run out]
Teddy Bear, Teddy Bear, climb the stairs
Teddy Bear, Teddy Bear, say your prayers
Teddy Bear, Teddy Bear, turn out the light
Teddy Bear, Teddy Bear, say goodnight

(New Mexico)

Teddy Bear, Teddy Bear, turn around
Teddy Bear, Teddy Bear, touch the ground
Teddy Bear, Teddy Bear, show your shoe
[jump on one foot]
Teddy Bear, Teddy Bear, how old are you?
1, 2, 3, etc.

(New York City)

I had a Teddy Bear dressed in green,
I didn't want it, so I gave it to the Queen.
The Queen didn't want it, so she gave it to the
    King,
And the King said:
Teddy Bear, Teddy Bear, turn around
Teddy Bear, Teddy Bear, touch the ground
Teddy Bear, Teddy Bear, look to the sky
Teddy Bear, Teddy Bear, wink one eye
Teddy Bear, Teddy Bear, touch your toes
Teddy Bear, Teddy Bear, out you goes

(New Zealand)

Teddy Bear, Teddy Bear, turn around
Teddy Bear, Teddy Bear, touch the ground
Teddy Bear, Teddy Bear, show your shoe
Teddy Bear, Teddy Bear, read the news
Teddy Bear, Teddy Bear, say your prayers
Teddy Bear, Teddy Bear, turn out the light
Teddy Bear, Teddy Bear, spell goodnight
G-O-O-D-N-I-G-H-T

(Pennsylvania)

Teddy Bear, Teddy Bear, turn around
Teddy Bear, Teddy Bear, touch the ground
Teddy Bear, Teddy Bear, touch your shoe
Teddy Bear, Teddy Bear, out goes you!

(Seattle)

Teddy Bear, Teddy Bear, turn around
Teddy Bear, Teddy Bear, turn around
Teddy Bear, Teddy Bear, get out of town

(Utah)

Teddy Bear, Teddy Bear, go upstairs, go upstairs
Teddy Bear, Teddy Bear, turn on the light, turn on
the light
Teddy Bear, Teddy Bear, brush your teeth, brush
    your teeth
Teddy Bear, Teddy Bear, say your prayers, say
    your prayers
Teddy Bear, Teddy Bear, go to bed, go to bed
    [if you think of more just add them]

(Wisconsin)

Mexico, Mexico,
Over the hills of Texaco,
Spanish dancers do the twist
Spanish dancers give a high kick
Spanish dancers turn around
Spanish dancers get out of town

(Delaware)

Dancers, dancers, do the split
Dancers, dancers, give a high kick
Dancers, dancers, do the kangaroo
Dancers, dancers, that will do
One, two, three, skidoo!

(Delaware)

Lady, Lady, drop your handkerchief
Lady, Lady, pick it up

*(England 1898; an early
ancestor)*

Butterfly, butterfly, fly around
Butterfly, butterfly, dip to the ground
Butterfly, butterfly, fold your wings tight
Butterfly, butterfly, flit out of sight

(New York)

Ladybug, ladybug, turn around
Ladybug, ladybug, touch the ground
Ladybug, ladybug, shine your shoes
Ladybug, ladybug, read the news
Ladybug, ladybug, how old are you?
1, 2, 3, etc.

(North Carolina)

Buster Brown, Buster Brown, turn around
Buster Brown, Buster Brown, touch the ground
Buster Brown, Buster Brown, touch your shoe
Buster Brown, Buster Brown, that will do!

(Toronto)

Johnny on the Ocean

*That infamous scoundrel Johnny, every innocent
girl's big brother, gets his just deserts in this
counting rhyme—proving that crime does not pay
and that little sisters can be dangerous (which no
doubt accounts for its great popularity). The
Philadelphia version is the fullest, but is clearly a
clever composite.*

Johnny on the ocean,
Johnny on the sea,
Johnny broke a bottle
And blamed it on to me.
I told Mama,
Mama told Papa,
Johnny got a whoopin' with a red-hot hopper.
What's the matter, Johnny?
A bee stung me.
Where at, Johnny?
On my knee.
Whyn't you catch it, Johnny?
It flies so fast.
Johnny went upstairs to play his drums.
He played so loud 'til the po-lice come.
Don't get me,
Get that white man under the tree.
He went to jail, just for fun,
To see old Johnny play his drum!

(Philadelphia)

Johnny on the ocean,
Johnny on the sea,
Johnny broke a dish
And blamed it on me.
I told Mama and Mama told Papa
And Papa told Mama
To give me some red hot peas!

(Alabama)

Johnny on the ocean,
Johnny on the sea,
Johnny broke a milk bottle
And blamed it on me.
I told Ma,
Ma told Pa,
Johnny got a whipping
And a ha! ha! ha!
How many whippings did he get?
1, 2, 3, etc.

(Chicago)

Cross the river,
Cross the sea
Johnny broke a milk bottle
And blamed it on me.
I told Ma, Ma told Pa,
Johnny got a whipping
And a Ha! Ha! Ha!
How many licks did he get?
1, 2, 3, etc.

(Georgia)

Johnny over the ocean,
Johnny over the sea,
Johnny broke a bean pot
        [a "teapot" in Massachusetts]
And blamed it onto me.
I told Ma,
Ma told Pa,
Johnny got a lickin'
Ha! Ha! Ha!
How many lickin's did
Johnny get?
1, 2, 3, etc.
(Maine)

Johnny over the ocean,
Johnny over the sea,
Johnny broke a sugar bowl
And blamed it onto me.
I told Ma, Ma told Pa.
Johnny got a licken,
Ha! Ha! Ha!
How many lickens
Did he get that week?
1, 2, 3, etc.

(Michigan)

Susie broke the milk bottle
And blamed it onto me.
I told Ma,
Ma told Pa.
Susie got a licking
So Ha! Ha! Ha!
How many lickings did she get?
1, 2, 3, etc.

*(Nebraska—home of the only bad
girl in the bunch)*

Down by the ocean,
Down by the sea,
Johnnie broke a milk bottle
And blamed it on me.
I told Ma and Ma told Pa.
Johnnie got a licking
With a Ha! Ha! Ha!
How many licks did he get?
1, 2, 3, etc.

*(North Carolina, Colorado,
New Mexico, and Utah)*

Johnny over the ocean,
Johnny over the sea,
Johnny broke a windee [window]
And he blamed it on me.
I told Ma,
Ma told Pa.
Johnny got a leathering,
Ha! Ha! Ha!

(Scotland)

Johnny broke a milk bottle,
I told Ma,
Ma told Pa.
Johnny got a lickin', so
Ha! Ha! Ha!

(Seattle)

Charlie over the ocean, Charlie over the sea,
Charlie broke a milk bottle
And blamed it on me.
I told Mamma,
Ma told Pa.
Charlie got a whipping,
So Ha! Ha! Ha!

(Tennessee)

Down in the Meadow

This rhyme was among those early four reported in the 1880's. It's still enormously popular, and is frequently used as a young girl's first expression of amorous fantasy.

The bullied elephant from North Carolina is a departure from the more common romantic theme, but he's one of my personal favorites.

The rhyme derives from a singing "ring game," and you must fill in the blanks with the names of the jumper and her Prince Charming.

Down in the meadow where the green grass grows,
There stands——with a horn and a nose.
She blows, she blows, she blows so sweet,
She calls——to kiss her sweet.

(Washington, D.C., 1886)

Down in the meadow where the corn cobs grow,
Fleas jumped on the elephant's toe.
Elephant cried, with tears in his eyes,
Why don't you pick on someone your size?

(North Carolina)

Down in the meadow where the green grass grow,
Sat little——
As sweet as a row.
Along came——
And kissed her on the nose.
O, ——, be ashamed!
Kissing a boy with an ugly name!
How many kisses did he give her?
1,2, 3, etc.

(North Carolina)

Down in the meadow where the green grass grows,
Sat little——
As sweet as a rose.
Along came a boy
And kissed her on the cheek.
Why,——, you ought to be ashamed!
Got a little boy friend and don't know his name!
What is his name?
A, B. C. etc.

Alabama

Down by the river where the green grass grows,
There sat——
As pretty as a rose.
She sang, she sang, she sang herself to sleep,
And up came——
And kissed her on the cheek.
How many kisses did he give her?
1, 2, 3, etc.

(Colorado)

Down in the meadow where the green grass grows,
There sat——
As sweet as a rose.
She sang, and she sang, and she sang so sweet,
Then along came——
And kissed her on the cheek.
How many kisses did she get?
1, 2, 3, etc.

(Delaware)

Down in the meadow where the green grass grows,
There stands——
As pretty as a rose.
Along comes——
And kisses her on the nose.
How many kisses did she receive?
1, 2, 3, etc.

(Maine)

Down in the valley where the green grass grows,
Sat little——,
Sweet as a rose.
Along came a billy goat and kissed her on the
nose.
Oh she let the billy goat kiss her on the nose!

(Nebraska)

Down in the meadow where the green grass grow,
Here come—— with her only go.
I said-a A,
I said-a B,
I saw a boy that I like on Sesame Street.
I saw him yesterday and I saw him again,
He gave me two kisses and a bottle of gin.
How many gins did I receive?
1, 2, 3, etc.

*(New York City—note the
contemporary twist)*

Down in the valley where the green grass grows
There sits——
Pretty as a rose.
Along came——
And kissed her on the cheek.
How many kisses did she get that week?
1, 2, 3, etc.

(Wisconsin)

Down in yonder meadow where the green grass
grows,
Where —— bleaches her clothes,
She sang, she sang, she sang so sweet,
She called her lover
At the end of the street.
He kissed her, he cuddled her
He put her on his knee,
And said, dearest ———'
I hope we will agree.
Agree, agree
I hope we will agree,
That we'll be married
At half past three!

(Scotland)

I'm a Little Dutch Girl

Like Teddy Bear, the little Dutch girl of this popular action rhyme has been known by many names. The Charlie Chaplin and Shirley Temple versions probably date from World War II. Although wartime references have not been dropped, many of today's jumpers admit they haven't the vaguest notion of what a submarine is.

Charlie Chaplin went to France
To teach the pretty girls
The hula dance.
First on heel,
Then the toe,
Do the splits
And around you go.
Salute to the Captain,
Curtsey to the Queen,
Touch the bottom of the submarine.

(Pennsylvania)

I'm a sailor girl
All dressed in blue.
These are the things I have to do:
Salute to the Captain,
Bow to the Queen,
Turn all around to the bald-headed King.

(Chicago)

Shirley Temple went to France
To teach the girls the Watusi dance.
First on heel, then on toe,
Split the rope and around she go.
Salute to the Captain,
Bow to the Queen
Touch the floor of the submarine.

(Chicago)

I'm a little Dutch girl
All dressed in blue.
And this is the duties
I must do each day:
Salute to the Captain,
March to the Queen,
And turn my back on a dirty submarine!

(Delaware)

Charlie Chaplin went to France
To show those French girls
How to dance.
First on the heel,
Then on the toe,
Round about and out you go.
Bow to the Captain,
Kneel to the Queen,
And give a salute to the big Marine.

(New York 1946)

Charlie Chaplin went to France
To teach the girlies how to dance.
Heel, toe, around we go,
Heel, toe, around we go.
Salute to the Captain,
Bow to the Queen,
Touch the bottom of a submarine and
KEEP THE KETTLE BOILING!

    [One jumper out and another in ON TIME,
    repeating the rhyme from the beginning.]

(New York 1960's)

I'm a little Dutch girl
Dressed in blue.
See all the actions I can do:
Salute to the Captain,
Bow to the Queen,
And turn my back on the dirty submarine.

(New York City 1974)

I'm a little Dutch girl
Dressed in blue.
Here are the things
I like to do:
Salute to the Captain,
Bow to the Queen,
Turn my back on the naughty, naughty King.
I can do the tap dance,
I can do·the split,
I can do the holka polka
Just like this.
1,2, 3, etc.

(North Carolina)

I'm a little Dutch girl
Dressed in blue.
These are the things
I like to do:
Salute to the King,
And bow to the Queen,
Turn on your tiptoes an twirl around.

(Philadelphia)

Charlie Chaplin went to France
To teach the ladies the crisscross dance.
First on heels,
Then on toes,
Around and around and around she goes.
S'lute to the King
And bow to the Queen,
And turn your back on the sour sardine.

(Seattle)

Shirley Temple went to France
To teach the ladies how to dance.
This is the dance she taught them first:
Heel, toe, around we go,
Heel, toe, around we go.
Salute to the Captain,
Bow to the King,
Make a dirty face at the ugly old Queen.

(Texas)

I'm a little Girl Guide [Girl Scout]
Dressed in blue.
These are the things I like to do:
Salute to the King,
Bow to the Queen,
Never turn my back on the Union Jack.
   (or)
Turn my back on the Old Tom cat.
Old Tom cat is very funny,
That's the way he makes his money.
Salt, mustard, ginger, pepper!
   (or)
Turn my back on the Sailor Jack.
Sailor Jack is very funny,
That's the way he earns his money.
Zoop la la
Zoop la la
Zoop, zoop, zoop! [Step on rope on last "zoop".]

(New Zealand)

Counting Rhymes

Rhymes by which to count kisses, bones, punches, squirts, bricks, flowers, doctors, and some other delightful nonsense. The counting is generally HOT PEPPER.

**A, my name is <u>Alice</u>
And my husband's name is <u>Arthur</u>.
We come from <u>Alabama</u>
Where we sell <u>Artichokes</u>!**

**B, my name is <u>Bridget</u>
And my husband's name is <u>Barney</u>.
We come from <u>Brooklyn</u>
Where we sell <u>Bicycles</u>!**

**C, my name is ——
And my husband's name is ——.
etc.** [this one is also a popular ball-bouncing
      rhyme]

A was an apple pie
B bit it
C cut it
D dealt it
E eats it
F fought for it
G got it
H had it
J joined it
K kept it
L longed for it
M mourned for it
N nodded at it
O opened it
P peeped in it
Q quartered it
R ran for it
S stole it
T took it
V viewed it
W wanted it
XYZ and apersand
All wished for a piece of land.

Bluebells, cockle shells,
Eevie ivy, over;
Mother went to market
To buy some meat;
Baby's in the cradle
Fast asleep.
The old clock on the mantle says
One o'clock, two o'clock . . . [to twelve o'clock.]

Chickety, chickety chop.
How many times before I stop?
1, 2, 3 . . .

Cinderella dressed in black
Went upstairs to peek through a crack.
How many people did she see?

Cinderella dressed in blue
Went upstairs to clean the flues.
How many flues did she clean?
    (or)
Went upstairs to use some glue.
How many bottles did she use?
    (or)
Went upstairs to shine her shoes.
How many shoes did she shine?

Cinderella dressed in brown
Went upstairs to make a gown.
How many stitches did she use?

    (or)
Went upstairs in her nightgown.
How many gowns did she wear?

Cinderella dressed in green
Went upstairs to have some dreams.
How many dreams did she have?

    (or)

Went upstairs to see a queen.
How many queens did she see?
    (or)

Went upstairs to fix the screens.
How many screens did she fix?
    (or)

Went upstairs to use some cream.
How many jars did she use?

Cinderella dressed in lace [Grace, grace,
                                          dressed in lace]
Went upstairs to powder her face.
How many boxes did she use?

Cinderella dressed in maroon
Went to the kitchen to make some macaroons.
How many macaroons did she make?
     (or)
Went upstairs to clean her room.
How many dustcloths did she use?
     (or)
Went upstairs to put on perfume.
How many bottles did she use?

Cinderella dressed in pink
Went upstairs to use the ink.
How many letters did she write?
     (or)
Went upstairs to wash the sink.
How many cleansers did she use?

Cinderella dressed in red
Went upstairs to make the bed.
How many covers did she use?
     (or)
Fell downstairs and bumped her head.
How many bumps did she get?

Cinderella dressed in rose
Went upstairs to powder her nose.
How many boxes did she use?

Cinderella dressed in white
Went upstairs to turn on the light.
How many light bulbs did she use?
     (or)
Went upstairs to see a knight.
How many knights did she see?
     (or)
Went outside to fly a kite.
How many kites did she fly?

Cinderella dressed in yellow
Went upstairs to kiss her fellow.
How many kisses did she give?
     (or)
Went downtown to buy an umbrella.
On the way she met her beau,
Who took her to a movie show.
How many kisses did she get?
     (or)
Went upstairs to kiss her fellow.
By mistake, she kissed a snake.
How many doctors did it take?

Dennis the Menace had a squirt gun,
He took it out and had some fun.
He shot a man in the boot.
How many squirts did he shoot?
    [when jumper misses]
Ooops! I'm out of water.

Eevie, ivy, over,
Here come the teacher with the hickory stick.
I wonder what I got for arithmetic.
One and one, two.
Two and two, four.
Now it's time for spelling.
Spell cat—C-A-T.
Spell rat—R-A-T.
George Washington never told a lie.
He ran around the corner and stole a cherry
    pie.
How many pies did he steal?

Hey,——! [jumper]
Somebody calling your name.
Hey,——!
Somebody playing your game.
I went downtown to listen to the clock.
It went tick tock, tick tock, one o'clock.
Tick tock, tick tock, two o'clock.
etc.

How many days has my baby to play?
1, 2, 3, etc.

I had a little brother
And his name was Johnny.
He played in the meadow
Where the frogs croaked clear.
He ran through the meadow
With a song on his tongue,
And he picked a few flowers for his mother.
How many flowers did he gather?

I had a little duck,
His name was Tiny Tim,
I put him in the bathtub
To see if he could swim.
He drank up all the water,
He ate up all the soap;
He died last night
With a bubble in his throat.
How many flowers did he have?

I know a boy and he is double-jointed.
He gave me a kiss, and I was disappointed.
He gave me another to match the other.
Now, now,——, I'll tell your mother.
How many kisses did you give him last night?

I love coffee, I love tea,
How many boys are stuck on me?

I was born in a frying pan.
Mother wants to know how old I am?
1, 2, 3, . . . [miss on your age]

Ke clip, ke clop, ke clip, ke clop,
A hundred times before we stop.
And if we trip, as trip we may,
We'll try again some other day!
1, 2, 3, . . . 99 [jumping to 100 is bad luck]

Kitty cat a bawlin'
And hurry up late.
1,2,3,4,5 and-a
1,2,3,4 and-a
1,2,3 and-a
1,2, and-a
1 and-a
Zero.

Lady, lady at the gate,
Eating cherries from a plate.
How many cherries did she eat?

My mother is a butcher,
My father cuts the meat.
I'm a little hot dog
Running down the street.
How many hot dogs do I sell?

Mother, Mother, I am sick,
Call the doctor quick, quick, quick!
Doctor, doctor, will I die?
Yes, my darling, by and by.
How many hours will I live?
        (or)
How many hearses will I have?

Not last night but the night before,
Twenty-four robbers came knocking at my
        door.
I went upstairs to get my gun,
You should have seen those robbers run!
He went east and he went west,
And he jumped over the cuckoo's nest.
How many robbers ran away?

Little Miss Pink,
Dressed in blue,
Died last night
At quarter past two.
Before she died
She told me this:
"When I jump rope
I always miss!"
Did she go up or down?
Up, down, up, down . . .

Mickey Mouse built a house.
How many bricks did he need?

My mother and your mother
Was hanging out clothes.
My mother socked your mother
Right in the nose.
How many punches did she get?

Peel an orange, round and round,
Peel a banana, upside down.
If you can count to twenty-four,
You may have an extra turn.

Polly on the railway
Picking up stones.
Along came an engine
And broke Polly's bones.
"Oh!" said Polly,
"That's not fair!"
"Oh!" said the engine driver,
"I don't care!"
How many bones did Polly break?

Teacher, teacher, oh so tired,
How many times were you fired?

Way down south where the sharecroppers grow,
I saw some croppers, croppin' to and fro.
They cropped some beans, they cropped some
    peas,
They cropped right up to the tops of the trees.
Up in Virginia where the grass grows green,
I saw a cute boy in a flyin' machine.
The machine went up, the boy came down,
He landed in the middle of Arling-town.
In North Carolina, where tobacco is the crop,
I saw an old hen go flippity-flop.
She flipped up once, she flipped down twice,
She landed in the middle of a bowl of rice.
In South Carolina where aristocrats grow,
I saw three birdies sittin' all in a row.
The crow said "caw," the cat said "cree,"
The finch said "now you all quit a-mockin' me."
Cree, craw, cree,
Cree, craw, cree,

"You all quit a-mockin' me."
Way down in Georgia where the peach trees blow,
I saw a little girl standin' on her tiptoe.
She tipped to the east, she tipped to the west,
She tipped to the boy that she loved best!
How many tippies did she make?
5, 10, 15, 20. . .

Prediction Rhymes

This group of rhymes is used to determine the jumper's sweetheart or future mate. Some clever jumpers will miss intentionally at a certain point, as a combination of wish fulfillment and a refusal to leave this crucial question to chance. In some places, the rhyme will be jumped twice, to determine first and last initials. Local custom may stigmatize the player who tries to jump through without missing, dubbing her an "old maid."

Red, white and blue,
    [run out and reenter BACK DOOR]
Stars shining over you.
Red, white and yellow,
Who is your fellow?
    or [for boys]
Red, white and green,
Who is your queen?
A,B,C,D. . . [PEPPER]

**Ipsey, Pipsy, tell me true,
Who shall I be married to?
A, B, C, . . . (1898)**

Apple jelly, my jam tart,
Tell me the name of your sweetheart?

**Dancing Dolly has no sense.
She bought some eggs for fifty-nine cents.
The eggs went bad and Dolly went mad.
A, B, C . . .**

Raspberry, raspberry, raspberry tart,
Tell me the initials of your sweetheart?

Strawberry, strawberry, strawberry jam,
Tell me the initials of my old man?

**Strawberry shortcake, cream on top,
Tell me the name of your sweetheart?**

Ice cream soda with a cherry on top,
Ginger ale or soda pop,
Tell me the initials of your sweetheart?

Ice cream, soda water, ginger ale, pop,
Tell me the initials of your sweetheart?

Ice cream soda and lemonade punch,
Tell me the name of your honeybunch?
(BARBADOS)

Ice cream soda, lemonade pop,
Tell me the initials of my sweetheart?

Ice cream soda, Delaware Punch,
Spell the initials of my honeybunch?
[When initial is determined,
see if he loves her:]
Yes, no, maybe so, certainly,
Yes, no, maybe so, certainly,
etc.

Milk shake, milk shake, cream on top,
Tell the initials of your sweetheart?

All in together
This is stormy weather,
Such a stormy weather.
January, February, March . . .
What date was you born on?
The first, the second, the third . . .
What day was you born on?
Sunday, Monday, Tuesday, Wednesday . . .
[This version determines your future mate by
birthdate]

Red, white, and yellow,
Have you got a fellow?
Yes, no, maybe so.
Yes, no, maybe so.
etc.

Bluebells, cockle shells [swaying rope]
Eevie, ivy, over. [start turning]
I like coffee, I like tea,
I like the boys and the boys like me.
Yes, no, maybe so.
etc.

Fire, fire, false alarm.
<u>Betty</u> fell in <u>Billy</u>'s arms. [fill in your own names]
First comes love, then comes marriage,
Then comes <u>Betty</u> with the baby carriage.
How many babies did she get that year?

<u>**Kevin**</u> **and** <u>**Susie**</u> **sitting in a tree,**
K-I-S-S-I-N-G.
First comes love, then comes marriage,
Then comes <u>**Susie**</u> **with a baby carriage.**
How many babies did she have?
How many bottles did she have?
How many diapers did she have?
etc.
[This rhyme and the one above can be used once
the sweetheart's identity has been determined]

Fortune Telling

*Here are some prediction rhymes where several
questions are strung together to give a more complete picture of what the future holds. This game
can be played with* ENDERS, *or with the player
jumping alone in the center of a circle while the
questions are chanted by the other players.*

*Fortune telling begins with one of the introduc-
tions (I), and goes on to several of the questions
(Q.) and answers, (A.) which are repeated until a
miss. If you use the "Gypsy, Gypsy" introduction,
use the first questions in each group. The second
questions are used with the second introduction.*

Introductions

I. Gypsy, Gypsy,
    Please tell me
    [repeat these lines before each question, for
example, "What my husband's going to be?" and
follow with one of the answers below, then repeat
"Gypsy, Gypsy, etc." and ask another question]

I. I love my Papa, that I do,
    And Mama says she loves him too.
    But Papa says he fears some day
    With some bad man I'll run away.
    [follow with one of the answers below, then
        with other questions and answers]

Questions and Answers

Q. What my husband's going to be?
Q. Who will I marry?
    A. Doctor, Lawyer, Bankerman, Thief,
        Rich man, Poor man, Indian Chief.
            (or)
    A. Rich man, Poor man, Beggar man,
        Thief, Doctor, Lawyer, Merchant,
        Chief, Tinker, Tailor, Soldier, Sailor
            (or)
    A. Rich man, Poor man, Beggar man,
        Thief, Doctor, Lawyer, Cowboy,
        Chief, A tinker, a tailor, a bow-legged
        sailor.
Q. What my ring is going to be?
Q. What kind of ring will I wear?
    A. Diamond, ruby, emerald, pearl.
            (or)
    A. Diamond, ruby, ten-cent ring.
Q. What my wedding dress will be?
Q. What kind of dress will I wear?
    A. Silk, satin, velvet, calico, rags! (1886)
            (or)
    A. Silk, satin, wool, leather.
            (or)
    A. Silk, satin, flour-bag, lace. (Barbados)

Q. What color my dress will be?
Q. What color will my dress be?
A. Pink, red, yellow, blue.
        (or)
A. Red, yellow, blue, white.

Q. What color suit is he going to wear?
    A. Red, blue, black, green.

Q. What kind of shoes am I going to wear?
    A. Clogs, slippers, boots, shoes.

Q. How am I going to the church?
    A. Bicycle, tricycle, motorcycle, car.
            (or)
    A. Taxi, wheelbarrow, cart, horse.

Q. What kind of flowers will I have?
    A. Roses, violets, carnations, weeds.

Q. What kind of house will I live in?
    A. Barn, pigpen, house, castle.
            (or)
    A. Upstairs, downstairs, broken-down
        house. (Barbados)
            (or)
    Big house, little house, pigpen, barn.

Q. How many children will I have?
    A. 1, 2, 3, etc.

Q. Will my children behave themselves?
    A. Yes, no, maybe so. Yes, no, maybe so,
        etc.

Multijump Rhymes

These rhymes call for two or more jumpers in the rope at the same time. There are some multijumper games on page 61

Two Jumpers

[1st jumper in]
Queen, queen,
Where did you get your chicken?
Queen, queen,
Where did you get your duck?
Queen, queen,
Where did you get your goat?

[1st jumper out; 2nd jumper in]
I got my chicken
Out of the yard.
I got my duck
Out of the pool.
I got my goat
Out of the garden.

[1st jumper in]
Cross the river, cross the lake,
I hope that ———— makes a bad mistake.
[2nd jumper in]
Cross the river, cross the lake,
I hope that ———— makes a bad mistake.
[repeat; last to miss gets HOT PEPPER]

[2 jumpers in; change
places on each count]
Changing bedrooms Number one!
[change]
Changing bedrooms Number Two!
[change]
Changing bedrooms Number Three!
[change]
Changing bedrooms Number Four!
[change, one jumper out, another in]

[for two jumpers]
Two in together,
This fine weather.
I spy Peter
Sitting on a heater.
Ding dong! The fire bell.
Up the ladder, down the ladder,
[jump from one end to the other]
January, February . . .

Four Jumpers

[1st jumper in]
Mother, Mother, I am ill,
Send for the doctor to give me a pill.
In came the doctor, [2nd jumper in]
In came the nurse, [3rd jumper in]
In came the lady with the alligator purse. [4th jumper in]

I don't want the doctor, [2nd out]
I don't want the nurse, [3rd out]
I don't want the lady with the [4th out]
   Big
   Fat
   Alligator purse!

Several Jumpers

[all jumpers in]
Everybody, everybody, come on in!
The first one to miss got to take an end!

[all jumpers in]
All in, a bottle of gin.
[all jumpers out]
All out, a bottle of stout.

[all jumpers in]
All in together,
Very fine weather.
I see teacher
Tapping on the winder.
Ding dong, fire drill.
January, February, March . . .
[run out on your birthday]

[run in, then out on your birthday]
Windy, windy weather,
They all jump in together.
January, February . . .
Windy, windy weather,
They all run out together.
January, February . . .

Call-In Rhymes

Here are rhymes where the jumper or those on line call out the name of the next player into the rope.

Also see the games "Best Friend" and "Calling In."

Room to rent, apply within.
When I move out, let——move in.

Calling in, calling out,
I call——in and out.

I like coffee, I like tea.
I'd like——to jump in with me.

Red, white and blue,
My mother caught the flu.
My father's lost his walking stick
And I blame you.
[point at the player you want to jump next]

On the mountain top stands a lady,
Who she is I do not know.
All she wants is gold and silver,
All she wants is a brand new beau.
Oh, come in, my——dear,
And out I shall go.

Vote, vote, vote for <u>Karen</u>, [jumper]
She'll call <u>Jane</u> to her door. [next jumper]
<u>Jane</u> is a dope,
'Cause she likes Bob Hope,
So we don't need <u>Karen</u> any more. [first jumper out]

Pop, pop, pop,
The girls are calling
For <u>Samantha</u> to come in.
<u>Samantha</u> is the one
Who is going to have the fun,
So we don't need—<u>Angela</u>!

Pump, pump, pump the door <u>Nancy</u>,
Calling <u>Linda</u> to the door.
Pump, pump, pump the door <u>Nancy</u>,
Calling <u>Linda</u> to the door.
   [Nancy runs out]

Pump, pump, pump the door <u>Linda</u>,
etc.

Every morning at eight o'clock,
You all may hear the postman's knock.
One, two, three, four.
There goes <u>Polly</u>.
   [jumper runs out and next player runs in ON TIME]

   [1st jumper in]
Early one morning, about eight o'clock,
What should I hear but the postman's knock.
Up jumps <u>Mary</u> to open the door;
   [1st jumper out; 2nd jumper in]
See how many letters on the floor?
One, two, three . . . [till jumper trips]
Boy, girl, boy, girl, etc. [writer's sex]
A,B,C, . . .   [initial of writer's 1st name]
A,B,C, . . .   [initial of writer's 2nd name]
This is a call-in prediction rhyme for two jumpers

Push Rhymes

In these rhymes, one jumper pushes or chases another out.

Granny in the kitchen,
Doin' some stitchin'
In comes the bogey man [2nd jumper in]
And chases Granny out! ["Granny" jumps out]

**Down the Mississippi,
Where the steamboats PUSH!**
 [2nd jumper pushes 1st out; this rhyme is also used when someone is hogging the rope]

California oranges,
Tap me on the back.
 [2nd jumper taps 1st, who runs out]

Action Rhymes

Action rhymes are challenging and fun. Create!

High Waters

**I asked my mother for fifteen cents
To see the elephant jump the fence.
He jumped so high he touched the sky,
And never came back till the Fourth of July.**
 [jump higher and higher]

**Fudge, fudge, call the judge.
Mama's got a brand new baby.
Ain't no girl, ain't no boy,
Just a plain ol' baby.
Hasn't any clothes so
Wrap it up in tissue paper,
Put it on the elevator.
First floor, miss!** [gradually raise rope]
**Second floor, Miss!
Third floor, Miss!
Fourth floor—
KICK IT OUT THE DOOR!**

When it rains the Mississippi River
Gets higher, and higher, and higher. [raise rope.]

Fancy Footwork

Down to the baker's shop
Hop, hop, hop. [one foot]
For my mother said
Buy a loaf of bread.
Down to the baker's shop
Hop, hop, hop.

Donald Duck is a one-legged, one-legged, one-legged duck. [one foot]
Donald Duck is a two-legged, two-legged, two-legged duck. [two feet]
Donald Duck is a three-legged, three-legged, three-legged duck. [two feet, one hand touches ground]
Donald Duck is a four-legged, four-legged, four-legged, duck. [two feet, both hands touch ground]
Donald Duck is a bow-legged, bow-legged, bow-legged duck.
Donald Duck is a pigeon-toed, pigeon-toed, pigeon-toed duck.
Donald Duck is a knock-kneed, knock-kneed, knock-kneed duck.
Donald Duck is a H-O-T duck. [HOT PEPPER until jumper misses]

Little Orphan Annie goes one foot, one foot.
Little Orphan Annie goes two feet, two feet.
Little Orphan Annie goes three feet, three feet. [one hand]
Little Orphan Annie goes four feet, four feet. [both hands]
Little Orphan Annie goes O-U-T out.

Girls, girls, had a fight,
Here comes Delores with a dress on tight!
She can wiggle, she can waggle,
She can do the split!
But I bet you five bucks she can't do this!
Lady hop with one foot, one foot, one foot.
Lady hop with two feet, two feet, two feet.

Annie, cum banny,
Tee alligo skanny,
T-legged,
Tie-legged,
Bow-legged Annie.

111

There was a crooked man, and he walked a
  crooked mile,
He found a crooked penny, beneath a crooked
  stile,
He bought a crooked cat that caught a crooked
  mouse,
And they all lived together in a little crooked
  house.
  [jump with feet crossed]

I went to Arkansas
To buy myself a saw.
I never saw so many saws
As I saw in Arkansas.
  [touch the ground each time you say "saw"]

On the next four rhymes, the trick is to catch the
rope between your legs.

Anna Banana
Played the piana.
All she knew was the Star Spangled Banner.
She wiggles, she waggles,
And does the split,
And when she misses, she misses like this. [catch
                                            rope]

Crackers, crackers,
Penny a cracker.
When you pull them
They go bang. [catch rope]

Miss, Miss, Little Miss, miss.
When she misses, she misses like this. [catch
  rope]

There was an old woman
And her name was Pat.
And when she died,
She died like that. [catch rope]
They put her in a coffin
And she fell through the bottom
Just like that. [catch rope]
They put her in a bed
And she bumped her head,
Just like that. [catch rope]

Imagin-Action

*Tricks, stunts, and pantomines of every
description.*

The wee wee woman and the wee wee man,
The wee wee kettle and the wee wee pan,
Said the wee wee woman to the wee wee man,
You take the kettle and I'll take the pan.
  [repeat with "medium sized," "tall tall," "fat
  fat," and "hopping"]

Up in the north
A long way off,
A donkey caught
The whooping cough.
What shall we give him
To make him better?
Salt, mustard, vinegar, pepper.
   [Salt = gradual crouching under lowering rope
   Mustard = turning around in a crouch
   Vinegar = turn in circle
   Pepper = fast]

Old man Dazy,
He went crazy.
Up the ladder [jump to one end]
Down the ladder [return backwards]
I say STOOP!
   [Stoop 3 counts and repeat]

   [swaying rope]
Old man Dazy, what makes you so lazy?
Up the ladder [jump to one end]
Down the ladder [return backwards]
   [full turning]
A,B,C, . . .
Salt, vinegar, mustard, pepper!! [increase speed]

Madam Morel,
She went to the well,
She never forgets her soap or towel.
She washes her hands,
And dries and dries,
She combs her hair,
She jumps up high,
And touches the sky,
Then twirls around
Until she drops.

Little Miss Pinkie, dressed in blue,
Died last night at half-past two.
Before she died, she told me this,
"Let the jump-rope miss like this."
   [miss in any way—trip,
   run out, straddle rope, etc.]

You gotta kick over, go side to side,
You gotta kick over, go side to side,
You gotta kick over, go side to side,
Turn around, touch the ground, side to side.

You gotta kick over, go side to side, [three
   times]
Touch your knees, touch your nose, side to side.

You gotta kick over, go side to side, [three
   times]
Turn around, touch the ground,
Touch your knee, touch your nose, side to side.

Two, four, six, eight,
Who do you appreciate?
I said-a 1,
I said-a 2 to the side
    [repeat 3 times, moving 3 steps]
I said-a 2,
I said-a 3 to the side
    [repeat 3 times, moving 3 steps left].
I said-a 3,
I said-a 4 to the side
    [repeat 3 times, moving 3 steps right]

Kick the bucket, baby,
One, two, three.
Kick the bucket, baby,
One, two, three.
Kick the bucket, kick the bucket, kick the bucket,
    baby
One, two, three.

Press your bellybutton,
One, two, three.
Press your bellybutton,
One, two, three.
Press your belly, press your belly, press your
bellybutton,
One, two, three.

Touch your head, baby,
One, two, three.
Touch your head, baby,
One, two, three.
Touch your head, touch your head, touch your
head, baby
One, two, three.

Jelly on the plate, jelly on the plate,
Wiggle-waggle, wiggle-waggle, [wiggle]
Jelly on the plate.

Sausage in the pan, sausage in the pan,
Turn it round, turn it round [turn]
Sausage in the pan.

Paper on the floor, paper on the floor,
Pick it up, pick it up [pick-up motion]
Paper on the floor.

Baby in the carriage, baby in the carriage,
Pull her out, pull her out [rock baby in arms]
Baby in the carriage.

Burglars in the house, burglars in the house,
Kick 'em out, Kick 'em out [kick]
Burglars in the house.

Last night, the night before,
A lemon and a pickle came a-knockin' at my door.
When I went down to let them in,
They hit me on the head with a rollin' pin.
This is what they said to me:
    Lady, lady turn around,
    Lady, lady touch the ground,
    Lady, lady show your shoe,
    Lady, lady how old are you?
    1, 2, 3, etc.

Last night or the night before,
Twenty-four robbers came knocking at the door.
As I ran out, they ran in, in, in [all players run
                                through]
Hit me on the head with a bottle of gin,
And this is what they told me:
    Spanish dancer do the split,
    The kick,
    The turn around, touch the ground,
    Run out the back door.

My mother and your mother
Live across the way—
Two-fourteen East Broadway.
Every night they have a fight
And this is what they say:
    Lady, lady turn around,
    Lady, lady touch the ground,
    Lady, lady touch your shoe,
    Lady, lady out goes Y-O-U.

Mrs. Brown went downtown,
She gave me a nickle to buy me a pickle,
The pickle was sour, she gave me a flower,
The flower was yellow, it got me a fellow,
The fellow was lazy, I gave him a slap,
The slap was hard, he gave me a card,
On the card it said:
    Spanish dancer does high kick,
    Spanish dancer does low split,
    Spanish dancer does low bow,
    Spanish dancer that'll do now.

I went downtown
To the alligator farm.
I sat on the fence
And the fence broke down. [stoop down]
The alligator bit me
By the seat of the pants
And made me do the houchi-kouchi dance.

Itiskit, itaskit, a green a yellow basket,
I lost a letter [drop handkerchief]
    for my mother and on my way
I found it, [pick up handkerchief]
I found it, I found it.

Hey, everybody,
Gather round Madison Town.
Like two up, [jump forward]
Two back, [jump backward]
False turn, [turn around]
Birdland, twice, [jump with feet crossed]
Kick that bird, [jump on one foot, kicking other
    foot]
Then spit that bird. [split]

Goosey, goosey, in a pot,
If you're hot,
Jump twenty-five times
And hop fifty times.

Charlie Chaplin walks like this.
Charlie Chaplin throws a kiss.
Charlie Chaplin winks one eye.
Charlie Chaplin waves good-bye.

   [swaying rope]
Bluebells, cockle shells,
Eevie, ivy, over!
   [full turning]
Dr. Brown is a very good man,
He teaches children all he can.
First to read and then to write,
Eevie, ivy, I pop out!

Raggedy Andy,
Sugar 'n' candy,
I pop in.

Raggedy Andy,
Sugar 'n' candy,
I pop down.

Raggedy Andy,
Sugar 'n' candy,
I pop up.

Raggedy Andy,
Sugar 'n' candy,
I pop out.

Blondie and Dagwood went downtown,
Blondie bought an evening gown,
Dagwood bought a pair of shoes,
Cookie bought the daily news.
And this is what it said to do:
Close your eyes and count to ten;
If you miss, take the end!

Postman, postman, do your duty.
Here comes [name of jumper]**, the American**
beauty.
She can wibble,
She can wobble,
She can do the split.
She can wear her dresses,
Way up to her hips.

Apple on a stick make me sick,
Make my stomach go too 'tirely sick.
Not because it's dirty; not because it's clean,
Just because I kissed a boy behind a magazine.
Girls, girls, how 'bout a fight?
Here come —— with her dress on tight.
    [name of jumper]
She can shake it, she can wreck it,
She can do the split.
I bet you five dollars she can't do this:
    [jumper names any stunt]

Up the ladder, down the ladder,
A-B-C.
Up the ladder, down the ladder,
H-O-T.

Up and down the city wall,
Penny loaf to feed us all.
I buy milk, you buy flour,
You shall have pepper in half an hour.
    [1898]

    [swaying rope]
Bluebells, cockleshells,
Eevie, ivy, over.
    [full turning]
You buy salt, and I'll buy flour,
And we'll bake a pudding
In half an hour
With salt, vinegar, mustard, pepper.

Sitting on the corner,
Chewing bubble gum.
Along came Jerry
And asked me for some.
I said, "I'd rather get a licking
Than give you some." [PEPPER]

Salt makes you thirsty,
Pepper makes you sneeze.
We'll make someone
Wobble at their knees.

Red hot bricks, [really fast]
Gotta get over what the leader's is
Or else you're out.

Pepsi-cola hits the spot.
Turn the rope and give her hot.
H-O-T spells HOT.

These two rhymes are good DOUBLE DUTCH.

Come here, Polly.
I'm gonna make you jolly
With this licking stick!

Two, four, six-eight, ten.
Two, four, six-eight, twenty.
Two, four, six-eight, thirty.
    (faster and faster to 100)

Bump Rhymes

Bump rhymes have "bump-words" on which the jumper must let the rope pass under the feet twice on one jump. For more about BUMPS, *see the glossary and the games section.*

You naughty <u>boy</u>,
You stole my <u>toy</u>,
You named it <u>Roy</u>,
You naughty <u>B</u>-<u>O</u>-<u>Y</u>.

What-oh, she <u>bumps</u>,
See how she <u>jumps</u>.
She jumps so <u>high</u>,
She nearly reaches the <u>sky</u>.

Robin Hood and his Merry <u>Men</u>
Went to school at half past <u>ten</u>.
Teacher said, "Late again!"
Robin Hood and his Merry <u>Men</u>.

Policeman, policeman, don't blame <u>me</u>,
Blame that boy behind the <u>tree</u>.
He stole sugar, he stole <u>tea</u>,
Policeman, policeman, don't blame <u>me</u>.

Cinderella at a <u>ball</u>,
Cinderella had a <u>fall</u>.
When she fell she lost her <u>shoe</u>,
Cinderella, <u>Y</u>-<u>O</u>-<u>U</u>.

In the Beatles' <u>school</u>
In Liver<u>pool</u>,
They learn their <u>yea</u>, <u>yea</u>, <u>yea</u>.

Chewing gum, chewing gum,
Penny per <u>packet</u>.
First you chew it,
Then you <u>crack it</u>.
Then you stick it
In your <u>jacket</u>.
Then your mother
Kicks up a <u>racket</u>.
Chewing gum, chewing gum,
Penny per <u>packet</u>.

[this one combines actions
with bump]
Oliver <u>jump</u>
Oliver <u>jump</u>
Oliver <u>jump</u> <u>jump</u> <u>jump</u>.

Oliver <u>kick</u>
Oliver <u>kick</u>
Oliver <u>kick</u> <u>kick</u> <u>kick</u>.

Oliver <u>twist</u>
Oliver <u>twist</u>
Oliver <u>twist</u> <u>twist</u> <u>twist</u>.

Oliver <u>jump</u> <u>jump</u> <u>jump</u>,
<u>Kick</u> <u>kick</u> <u>kick</u>,
<u>Twist</u> <u>twist</u> <u>twist</u>.

Hot Rhymes

*Forgetful Mabel, armed with a full bag of
seasonings and spices, has been keeping
jumpers on their toes since the turn of the century.*

Mabel, Mabel, set your table,
And don't forget your red hot peas!

Mabel, Mabel, set the table,
Don't forget the salt and pepper.

**Mabel, Mabel, set the table,
Don't forget the red hot pepper.**

Mabel, Mabel, set the table,
Don't forget the salt, vinegar, mustard, pepper,
Ceedar, cider, red hot pepper!

Mabel, Mabel, set the table,
Don't forget the salt, pepper, vinegar, hot.
[In Wisconsin and Nebraska,
as in France, "Vinegar" is really fast, and "hot"
still faster]

Mabel, Mabel, set the table,
Put on salt, pepper, vinegar.
Mabel, Mabel, clean the table,
Take off vinegar, pepper, salt.

Easy, greasy, take it easy;
Salt, pepper, vinegar, hot.

   [swaying rope]
Baker, baker, bake your bread.
   [full turning]
Salt, vinegar, mustard, pepper.

Onery, twoery, threery, same,
Bottle of vinegar,
Who'll be game?
Salt, mustard, vinegar, pepper.

One to make ready and two to prepare,
Good luck to the rider,
Away goes the mare.
Salt, mustard, vinegar, pepper.

Knife and fork, lay the cloth,
Bring me up a leg of pork.
Don't forget the salt,
Mustard, vinegar, pepper.
   [1898]

Foreign Rhymes

For most of the foreign rhymes in this group we can thank Professor Francelia Butler.

Generalizing about her large collection of jump-rope rhymes, she concluded that "vigorous athletic rhymes" come largely from Scandinavia, Germany, and other northern countries. Rhymes of "religious and domestic life, particularly food," come from Spain, Portugal, Italy, and many Latin and South American countries.

"Lovely, poetical rhymes" come from the East, Laos, Israel, and India.*

Split peas and rice is very nice
Upon a rainy day.
And when you go to blow the fire,
The spark will come and burn you.
Tol-en, tol-en, tol-en-to-tol-en dee.

(Barbados)

The porch of my house is not special.
When it rains it gets wet like the rest.
Squat girl, squat again.
If you can't squat, you can't play.

(Cuba)

A little coach driver
Asked me last night,
If I would like to have a ride.

And I told him,
With lots of thanks,
That I get seasick
Riding in coaches.

(Dominican Republic)

And Santa, and Santa
And Santa Teresa told me,
By word, by word
By word of Saint Ramón,
That every, that every
That every man has
A head, a head,
A head of sausage
And feet, and feet
And feet like a rat.

(Ecuador)

The clown in his store
On the palace stair,
Teaching numbers
To his pupils there.
1, 2, 3, etc.

(France)

---

*Francelia Butler, "International Variations in Skip-Rope Rhymes," *ellessee Folklore Society Bulletin, 31,* 1965.

O, the salad!
When it grows up,
People will eat it
With oil
And vinegar! ["Vinegar" = Hot Pepper]

(France)

1, 2, 3, 4, 5, 6, 7,
Where is my girl friend living?
She's not here, she's not there,
She must be in America.

(Germany)

How can I hurt my mother
And make her so upset?
She sings all day,
And every night
She treats me like her pet.

(Greece)

Behind the mountain,
One, two, three,
Three dwarfs were sitting,
One, two, three.
They didn't eat, they didn't drink,
Just sat there chatting,
One, two, three.

(Israel)

Scattered and gleaming on the ground, like the full
  moon,
Are sampots perfect and innumerable.
Sampots of every color . . .
Some are even yellow.

(Laos)

Adorned with egrets and with mother-of-pearl
  inlaid,
The palaces shine like golden stars.
The queen is named Canda, graceful as any
  drawing.

(Laos)

Little rope, little rope, oh my little rope,
Unwind yourself from the round ball;
Twirl round and round and high.
Take me outdoors to the air and the sun.
Out of the room, out of the house, the narrow
  house.
Nobody can catch us!
Little rope, little rope, oh my little rope,
Unwind yourself from the ball.

(Luxembourg)

This old rhyme, which was set to music in "Stop the World, I want to Get Off," has one version for girl jumpers and another for the boys.

GIRLS

My mother said
I never should
Play with the gypsies
In the wood.
If I should
She would say,
"Naughty girl to disobey,
Disobey, disobey,
Naughty girl to disobey."
I wish my mother would
Hold her tongue.
She had a boy
When she was young.
I wish my father would
Do the same.
He had a girl
With an awful name.

BOYS

My mother said
I never should
Play with gypsies
In the wood.
The wood was dark,
The grass was
    green,
In came Sally
With a tambourine.
I went to the sea,
No ship to get across;
I paid ten shillings
For a blind white horse.
I was up on his back
And was off in a crack.
Sally told my mother
I would never come back.

(Northern Ireland)

My wee brother is no good.
Chop him up for firewood.
When he's dead, cut off his head,
Make it into gingerbread.

(Northern Ireland)

Eni, eni, mino, mo,
Set the baby on the po. ["pot"]
When it's done,
Clean its bum,
And give it a lump
Of sugar plum.

(Northern Ireland)

Georgie and Jack are dressed in black,
Silver buckles behind their backs.
Foot for foot, knee for knee,
"Turn back Georgie and come with me."
"I have a leg for a stocking,
I have a foot for a shoe,
I have a kiss for a bonny wee lass,
But I have none for you."

(Northern Ireland)

Dear Baby Jesus,
I want a plane soon.
Or an automobile,
Or a big balloon.
Or a motor boat
That's neat and snappy.
Any old thing
And I'll be happy!

(Portugal)

Kilty Kilty Calder
Couldn't play his drum;
His mother took the bellows
And blew him up the lum. ["chimney"]

I came to a river, I couldn't get across.
I paid ten shillings for an old blind horse.
I jumped on its back and its bones went crack.
We all played the fiddle till the boat came back.
The boat came back, we all jumped in.
The boat capsized, and we all fell in.

[Compare this Scottish rhyme to the Northern Irish
"My mother said I never should" for an example
of the way rhymes change with time and
geography.]

(Scotland)

1, 2, 3, 4, 5, 6, 7.
I don't want to be a baker's wife.
But a smith, yes, a smith,
Do I want to hammer with?

(Sweden)

Katherina, Barbara,
Look how you've cared for the house!
A chicken's been stolen,
The feathers all plucked,
Eaten, no doubt, in Ljubljana!

(Yugoslavia)

Early Rhymes

The origins of these rhymes in singing games, folk ballads, and other verse forms go back at least a hundred years, and in some cases, much further.

All in together, girls,
No mind the weather, girls.
I spy a lark, sitting in the dark.

[This French rhyme comes
from the sixteenth century.]
Pan, pan, pan,
Mama is at Caan.
I've eaten ten eggs,
The heads of two cows,
A hundred pounds of bread,
And still I am hungry!

I had a little nut tree,
Nothing would it bear
But a silver nutmeg
And a golden pear.
The King of Spain's daughter
Came to visit me,
And all because
Of my little nut tree.
[Ms. Butler calls this rhyme "one of the oldest and naughtiest. Legend has it that it was the veiled protest of the people to Henry VIII's courtship of Catherine of Aragon and later, to the future King Charles I's interest in the Infanta of Spain."]*

The following rhymes were all used as jumping rhymes in the nineteenth century.

House to let, apply within,
People turned out for drinking gin.
Smoking pipes is a terrible sin,
So—— runs out and——runs in.

I like coffee, I like tea,
I like boys and boys like me.
I'll tell my mother when I get home
The boys won't let the girls alone.

When I was young and able
I sat upon the table.
The table broke
And gave me a poke,
When I was young and able.

Up and down the ladder wall,
Ha'penny loaf to feed us all.
A bit for you, and a bit for me,
And a bit for Punch and Judy.

Up and down the ladder wall,
In and out "The Eagle."
That's the way the money goes,
Pop goes the weazle.

---

*Francelia Butler, *The Skip-Rope Book* (New York: Dial Press, 1963).

Half a pound of two-penny rice,
Half a pound of treacle.
Penny worth of spice
To make it nice,
Pop goes the weazle.

Dancing Dolly had no sense,
For to fiddle for eighteen pence.
All the tunes that she could play
Were "Sally get out of the donkey's way."

Cups and saucers
Plates and dishes,
My old man wears
Calico breeches.

B-L-E-S-S-I-N-G.
Roses red, roses white,
Roses in my garden.
I would not part
With my sweetheart
For tuppence, ha 'penny, farthing.
A, B, C, etc.

Plain Old Rhymes

These rhymes can be used in many ways and many combinations.
As they stand, they delighfully defy description.

Long Ones

[The first four lines are repeated before each verse.]
My girl's a corker,
She's a New Yorker,
I'd do most anything
To keep her in style.

She's got a pair of feet
Just like two plates of meat.
That's where all my money goes.
Umpa umpa umpa pa pa
Umpa umpa umpa pa pa.

She's got a pair of shoulders
Just like two great big boulders.
That's where all my money goes.
Umpa . . .

She's got a pair of hips
Just like two battleships.
That's where all my money goes.
Umpa . . .

She's got a great big nose
Just like a fireman's hose.
That's where all my money goes.
Umpa . . . .

She's got a pair of eyes
Just like two custard pies.
That's where all my money goes.
Umpa . . .

She's got a head of hair
Just like a grizzly bear.
That's where all my money goes.
Umpa . . . .

She's got a pair of legs
Just like two whiskeykegs.
That's where all my money goes.
Umpa . . .

She's got a pair of lips
Just like two greasy chips.
That's where all my money goes.
Umpa . . .

I am a little Dutch girl,
As pretty as pretty can be.
And all the boys around my way
Are crazy over me.
My boyfriend's name is Chiclet,
He comes from Alabam,
With a pickle on his nose
And turned down toes,
And that's the way my story goes.
He gave me some peaches,
He gave me some pears,
He gave me a dirty kiss
And knocked me down the stairs.
I gave him back his peaches,
I gave him back his pears,
I gave him back his dirty kiss
And knocked him down the stairs.
My mother need those peaches,
My mother need those pears,
My mother saw that dirty kiss
And kicked us down the stairs.

I went downtown to see Miss Brown,
She gave me a nickel to buy a pickle.
The pickle was sour so I bought a flower.
The flower was dead so I bought some bread.
The bread was thin so I bought a pin.
The pin was sharp so I bought a harp,
And on this harp I played:
I'm a little Dutch girl dressed in white,
These are the things I do at night:
Comb my hair, brush my teeth, say my
prayers,
Jump into bed and go to sleep.

Dream Lover, where are you?
Upstairs on the toilet stool.
Whatcha doing way up there?
Washing out my underwear.
How'd you get them so clean?
With a bottle of Listerine.
Where'd you get the Listerine?
From a can of pork and beans.
Where'd you get the pork and beans?
In the city of New Orleans.
How'd you get way down there?
'Cause I killed a polar bear.
Why'd you kill the polar bear?
'Cause he dirtied my underwear.
I want a Dream Lover,
Never have to dream alone.
[This one is a parody of a rock and roll hit of 1958]

What are you doing here, sir?
Drinking up the beer, sir.
Where did you get the beer, sir?
It wasn't far nor near, sir.
    Yes, sir, no, sir.
    I must be on my way, sir.
Where did you leave your cane, sir?
Down in Lover's Lane, sir.
What were you doing there, sir?
None of your affair, sir.
    Yes, sir, no, sir,
    I must be on my way, sir.
Why do you speak so bold, sir?
Because I have a cold, sir.
Where did you get the cold, sir?
Up at the North Pole, sir.
    Yes, sir, no, sir,
    I must be on my way, sir.
Where do you go to church, sir?
Down by yonder birch, sir.
Perhaps we then shall meet, sir?
If I must rest my feet, sir.
    Yes, sir, no, sir,
    I must be on my way, sir.
Have you a horse to ride, sir?
I'm sitting on its hide, sir.
But no mount I see, sir.
Its hide is sewed on me, sir.
    Yes, sir, no, sir,
    I must be on my way sir.
When will you be gone, sir?
At the crack of dawn, sir.
Who will let you out, sir?
My musket good and stout, sir.

Yes sir, no, sir,
I must be on my way, sir.
Pray, what is your name, sir?
My name is: [jump the letters of your name]

Mother, Mother, have you heard,
Papa's going to buy me a mocking bird!
If that mocking bird don't sing,
Papa's going to buy me a diamond ring.
If that diamond ring turns brass,
Papa's going to buy me a looking glass.
If that looking glass gets broke,
Papa's going to buy me a billy goat.
If that billy goat runs away,
Papa's going to buy me a load of hay.
If that load of hay gets wet,
Papa's going to whip me until I sweat.

Down at the station, early in the morning,
See the little daffodils all in a row.
See the little driver turn the little handle,
Choo, choo, toot, toot, off they go.
Down at the station, early in the morning,
See the little pufferbellys all in a row.
See the station master pull the little handle,
Toot, toot, puff, puff, off they go.

I'm a little orphan girl,
My mother she is dead.
My father is a drunkard
And won't buy me my bread.

I sit upon the window sill
To hear the organ play,
And think of my dear mother,
Who's dead and far away.

Ding dong the castle bell,
Farewell to my mother.
Bury me in the old churchyard,
Beside my eldest brother.

My coffin shall be white,
Six little angels by my side,
Two to sing, and two to play,
And two to carry my soul away.
[This Scottish rhyme is popular
  for GERMAN ROPES]

I am brown, cocoa brown,
People stamp me in the ground.
I'm a nut, I'm a nut,
So are you, so are you.

I called myself on the phone,
Asked myself if I was home,
Asked myself for a date,
Have to be ready at half past eight.
I'm a nut, I'm a nut,
So are you, so are you.

I love myself, I love myself,
Took myself to a picture show,
Wrapped my arms around my waist,
Got so fresh I slapped my face.
I'm a nut, I'm a nut,
So are you, so are you.

And Not So Long Ones

Salome was a dancer,
She danced before the king.
She danced hanky-panky
And she shimmied everything.
The king said, "Salome,
You can't do that in here!"
Salome said, "Baloney!"
And kicked the chandelier!

Three little bad boys dressed in white,
Wanted to go to Harvard on the tail of a kite.
The kite string broke and down they fell,
They didn't go to Harvard, they went to . . .
Now don't get excited, and don't turn pale,
They didn't go to Harvard, they went to Yale.

I had a little monkey,
I sent him to the country,
I fed him gingerbread.
He jumped out the window,
And broke his little finger,
And now my monkey's dead.

I had a little monkey dressed in red,
Along came a train and knocked him dead.
I called for the doctor,
I called for the nurse,
I called for the lady with the big fat purse.
"He's dead," said the doctor.
"He's dead," said the nurse.
"He's dead," said the lady with the big fat purse.

Acca bacca boom a cracka,
Acca bacca boo.
If your daddy chews tobacca,
He's a dirty do.
O-U-T spells out.
Out goes a rat.
Out goes a cat.
Out goes a lady with a see-saw hat.

Dickey had a brother,
His name was Tiny Tim,
He put him in the bathtub
To see if he could swim.
He drank up all the water,
He ate up all the soap,
He tried to eat the bathtub,
But it wouldn't fit down his throat.
Miss Lucy called the doctor,
The doctor called the nurse,
The nurse called the lady
With the alligator purse.

Mother, mother, I am ill,
Call the doctor over the hill.
In came the doctor,
In came the nurse,
In came the lady
With the alligator purse.
"Measles," said the doctor.
"Mumps," said the nurse.
"Nothing," said the lady
With the alligator purse.

Grandma, grandma, sick in bed,
She called the doctor and the doctor said:
Grandma, grandma, you're not sick.
All you need is a big fat kick.

[jump to one end of the rope]
Mother, mother, where's the key?
Go ask father. [jump to the other end]
Father, father, where's the key?
Have you done the dishes?
Yes.
Have you swept the floor?
Yes.
Have you done your school work?
Yes.
Turn the key in the lock and run out to play.
[A form of this little game
was known in the 1890's]

This is the way you spell "Tennessee."
One asee, two asee, three asee,
Four asee, five asee, six asee,
Seven asee, eight asee, nine asee,
Tennessee!

One bright morning in the middle of the night,
Two dead boys got up to fight.
Back to back they faced each other,
Drew their swords and shot each other.
Two deaf policemen heard the noise,
Came and shot the two dead boys.
If you don't believe that this is true,
Ask the blind man, he saw it too!

Mother, mother, what is that,
Hanging down that lady's back?
Hush, my child, you naughty thing!
That's the lady's corset string!

Ladies and gentlemen
Children too,
There's a little girl
Going looking for you.
Hands up, torch-a-torch.
Two years old, goin' on three,
Wear my dresses upon my knee.
Sister has a boyfriend,
Comes every night;
Walks in the parlor
And turns out the light.
Peep through the keyhole,
What did I see?
Johnny Johnny, Johnny,
Put your arms around me.

My sister Bunny walks very funny,
For she isn't very steady on her feet.
She spends all her money
Drinking with her honey
In the bar on the corner of the street.

I went upstairs to make my bed,
I made a mistake and bumped my head.
I went downstairs to milk my cow,
I made a mistake and milked the sow.
I went in the kitchen to bake a pie,
I made a mistake and baked a fly.

Downtown, baby,
Down by the roller coaster.
Sweet, sweet baby,
I never let you go.
Shimmy, shimmy coco bop,
Shimmy, shimmy down.
Shimmy, shimmy coco bop,
Shimmy, shimmy down.

I been told when a boy kiss a girl,
Take a trip, around the world, hey, hey!
Shak-a-doo-bop.
1, 2, 3, 4, 5, 6, 7, 8, 9, 10.

Hawaiian Punch, going up,
Hawaiian Punch, going down,
Hawaiian Punch is a colored boy,
He goes all around the town.
1, 2, 3, 4, 5, 6, 7, 8, 9, 10.

Here comes Uncle Jessie
Ridin' through the woods,
And silver horse and buckles,
And buckles on his shoes.
Now if he was a fella,
I tell you what to do:
Just take some salt and pepper,
And put it in your shoe.
All gone girl, shake that sugar.
All gone girl, shake that sugar.
Shake it to the east,
Shake it to the west,
Shake it to the very one
That you love the best.

The devil flew from north to south,
With (my teacher) in his mouth.
And when he found she was a fool,
He dropped her on the ———— School.

Whistle, while you work,
Jenny made a shirt.
Jessie wore it, Bessie tore it,
Mary made it worse!

Minnie, Minnie HaHa
Went to see her Pa Pa.
Pa Pa died, Minnie cried,
Minnie, Minnie HaHa.

Sally drinks lemonade,
Sally drinks beer,
Sally drinks other things
That make her feel so queer.
"Ooops," says the lemonade,
"Ooops," says the beer,
"Ooops," say the other things
That make her feel so queer.

Lincoln, Lincoln, I've been thinkin'
What on earth have you been drinkin'?
Looks like water, smells like wine,
Oh, my gosh! It's turpentine.
10, 20, 30 . . . to 100 [then HOT PEPPER]

Archie, Archie, how about a date?
Meet me around the corner
At a quarter to eight.
First comes love,
Then comes marry,
Here comes Sally with a baby carriage.

John and Mary
Up in a tree,
K-I-S-S-I-N-G.
First comes love,
Then comes marriage,
Then comes Mary
With a baby carriage.

Postman, postman,
Do your duty.
Send this letter
To my cutie.
Don't you stop
Nor don't delay.
Get it to her
Right away.

Fireman, fireman,
Number Eight,
Hit his head against the gate.
The gate flew in, the gate flew out,
That's the way he put the fire out.
O-U-T spells out—
And out you go.

Doctor Foster
Went to Gloucester,
In a shower of rain.
He stepped in a puddle
Way up to his middle
And never went there again.

All in together,
All sorts of weather,
I spy Jack
Peeping through a crack.
Bang, shot, fire.

All in together,
This fine weather,
I saw a peacock
Sitting on the window.
Fish, bang, fire, out.

The autumn is Bo-Peep,
The milkweed pods her sheep.
Alas! She cannot find them.
For where they stood a while ago
She finds all hanging in a row,
They've left their tails behind them.

Bake a pudding, bake a pie.
Did you ever tell a lie?
Yes you did, I know you did.
You broke your mother's teapot lid.
O-U-T spells out,
And out you must go,
Right in the middle
Of the deep blue sea.

A bottle of pop, a big banana,
We're from southern Louisiana.
That's a lie, that's a fib,
We're from Colorado.

Eggs, butter, cheese, bread,
Stick, stock, stone dead.
Set him up, set him down,
Set him in the old man's crown.

I am a little girl, just so high.
I can make donuts, I can make pie.
I broke a platter right in two,
Mother came to whip me,
Boo, hoo, hoo.

[To the tune of "K-K-K-Katie"]
Inky-pinkie, skinny-ma-linkie,
Andy-Pandy, Pandy-Andy, bandy boots.
Over-dover, dover-rover,
Andy-Pandy, Pandy-Andy, bandy boots.

Intery, mintery, cutery corn,
Apple seed and apple thorn.
Wire, briar, limber lock,
Three geese in a flock
Sit and sing by the spring.
O-U-T spells out,
With a dirty dishrag wrapped around your snout!
Over yonder steep hills,
There my father dwells.
He has jewels, he has rings,
And very many pretty things.
Strike Jack, like Tom,
Blow the bellows, Black Finger,
Out—of—the—game.

I want a teddy bear,
With blue eyes and curly hair;
Up among the Eskimos,
Having a game of dominoes.

I wish tonight was Saturday night,
Tomorrow will be Sunday.
I'll be dressed in all my best,
To go out with my Johnny.

Eenie, meenie, tipsy, teeny,
Apple jack, Paul Sweeny.
Dotchy, potchy, Don Morotchy,
Oh, par, dar, see,
Out goes Y-O-U.

Johnny Maloney,
Stick, stock, stony.
Highballa, o balla,
Johnny Maloney.

A lady in a boat
With a red petticoat,
And her name is—MISS!

Little Sally Ann,
Sittin' in a pan,
Weepin' and a cryin'
For a nice young man.
Rise, Sally, rise.
Wipe your dirty eyes.
Turn to the east, turn to the west,
Turn to the very one that you love best.

Mary Mack, Mack, Mack
All dressed in black, black, black
With silver buttons, buttons, buttons
All down her back, back, back.

Mickey Mouse bought a house,
Couldn't pay the rent
And got kicked out.

My Aunt Jane she called me in,
She gave me tea out of her little tin.
Half a bun and sugar on the top,
Three sugar lumps out of her little shop.
My Aunt Jane she's awful smart,
She bakes little rings in an apple tart.
And when Halloween comes around,
Beside that tart I'm always found.

Oh, Tommy, I am ashamed of you,
For leaving little Chrissie across the ocean blue.
Her heart is nearly broken, she's dying for a
**   kiss,**
Oh, Tommy, I am ashamed of this!

Old King Cole was a merry old soul,
He tried to get to heaven
On a telephone pole.

Once I saw a little bird
Come hop, hop, hop;
So I cried ''Little bird,
Will you stop, stop, stop?''
And was going to the window
To say, ''How do you do?''
But he shook his little tail,
And far away he flew.

Red-headed sapsucker,
Sitting on a vine.
Wants a chew of 'bacca,
But he won't get mine!

Red-headed sapsucker,
Sitting on a fence,
Trying to make a dollar
Out of fifteen cents!

Standing at the bar
Smoking a cigar,
Riding on a donkey,
Ha, ha, ha.
Take my arm,
I do no harm,
I only smoke a cigar.

The wind, the wind, the wind blows high,
The rain comes tumbling from the sky.
Little Barbara says she'll die
If she doesn't get a man with a rosy eye.
She is handsome, she is pretty,
She is a girl from New York City.
A knock at the door and a ring at the bell;
Ah, my true love, are you well?

One, two, three, four,
Mother washed the kitchen floor.
Floor dried, Mother cried,
One, two, three, four.

One, two, three,
The bumblebee.
The rooster crows
Out goes she.

**Two, four, six, eight,
Don't make love at the garden gate.
Cause love is blind
But the neighbors ain't.**

You can fall from a steeple,
You can fall from above,
But for heaven's sake, Samantha,
Don't fall in love!

Index of First Lines

Index of Games

Bibliography

*Abrahams, Roger D. *Jump-Rope Rhymes, A Dictionary*. Austin: University of Texas Press, 1969.

————"Some Jump-Rope Rimes from South Philadelphia," *Keystone Folklore Quarterly,* 8 (1963).

Adams, Edwin H. *Jump-Rope Rhymes*. Seattle: Silver Quoin Press, 1947.

*Ainsworth, Catherine H. "Jump Rope Verses Around the United States," *Western Folklore,* 20 (1961).

Babcock, W. H. "Games of Washington Children," *American Anthropologist,* 1(1888).

Bett, Henry. *The Games of Children; Their Origin and History*. London: Methuen & Co., 1929.

Brewster, Paul G. *American Nonsinging Games*. Norman: University of Oklahoma Press, 1953.

Buckley, Bruce R. "Jump-Rope Rhymes: Suggestions for Classification and Study," *Keystone Folklore Quarterly*, 11(1966).

Burroughs, Margaret Taylor. *Did You Feed My Cow? Street Games, Chants and Rhymes*. Chicago and New York: Follett Publishing Co., 1969.

Butler, Francelia. "International Variations in Skip-Rope Rhymes," *Tennessee Folklore Society Bulletin*, 31(1965).

*_____."'Over the Garden Wall/I Let the Baby Fall . . .'," *The New York Times Magazine*, December 16, 1973.

Butler, Francelia, and Gail Haley. *The Skip Rope Book*. New York: The Dial Press, 1963.

Clark, Mary Olmsted. "Song Games of Negro Children in Virginia," *Journal of American Folklore*, 3(1890).

Cooper, Kenneth H., M.D. *Aerobics*. New York: Bantam Books, 1968.

*_____*The New Aerobics*. New York: Bantam Books, 1970.

*Cooper, Mildred, and Kenneth H. Cooper, M.D. *Aerobics for Women*. New York: Bantam Books, 1973.

Darling, Robert C., M.D., and John A. Downey, M.D. *Physiological Basis of Rehabilitation Medicine*. Philadelphia, London and Toronto: W.B. Saunders Co., 1971.

Depew, Arthur M. *The Cokesbury Game Book*. New York: Abingdon Press, 1960.

Forbush, William B., and Harry Allen. *The Book of Games for Home, School, and Playground*. Philadelphia and Toronto: John C. Winston Co., 1954.

Gomme, Alice Bertha. *The Traditional Games of England, Scotland, and Ireland, Vol.* II. New York: Dover Publications, 1964.

Hall, Sue. "That Spring Perennial—Rope Jumping!," *Recreation*, March, 1941.

Hawthorne, Ruth. "Classifying Jump-Rope Games," *Keystone Folklore Quarterly*, 11(1966).

*Nulton, Lucy. "Jump Rope Rhymes as Folk Literature," *Journal of American Folklore*, 61(1948).

*Prentup, Frank B. *Skipping the Rope for Fun and Fitness*. Boulder, Colorado: Pruett Publishing Co., 1963.

*Ritchie, James T.R. *The Golden City*. Edinburgh and London: Oliver & Boyd, Ltd., 1965.

Sone, Violet West. "Rope Jumping Jingles," *Backwoods to Border,* publication of the Texas Folklore Society, Vol. 18, 1943.

*Sutton-Smith, Brian. *The Folkgames of Children*, publication of the American Folklore Society, Vol. 24. Austin and London: University of Texas Press, 1972.

Of special interest.